1990

Break All Rules!
Punk Rock and the
Making of a Style

Studies in the Fine Arts: The Avant-Garde, No. 68

Stephen C. Foster, Series Editor

Professor of Art History
University of Iowa

Other Titles in This Series

Break All Rules!
Punk Rock and the Making of a Style

by
Tricia Henry

 Research
Press
Ann Arbor / London

Produced and distributed by
UMI Research Press
an imprint of
University Microfilms Inc.
Ann Arbor, Michigan 48106

Library of Congress Cataloging in Publication Data

Henry, Tricia, 1955–
   Break all rules! : punk rock and the making of a style / by Tricia
Henry.
      p. cm.—(Studies in the fine arts. Avant-garde ; no. 68)
      Bibliography: p.
      Includes index.
      ISBN 0-8357-1980-4 (alk. paper)
      1. Punk rock music—History and criticism. I. Title.
   II. Series.
   ML3534.H46   1989
   781.66—dc20   89-30474
                                                                         CIP
                                                                          MN

British Library CIP data is available.

The paper used in this publication meets the minimum requirements of
American National Standard for Information Sciences—Permanence of Paper for Printed
Library Materials, ANSI Z39.48-1984. ∞ ™

Contents

Preface

Rock-and-roll is a relatively new phenomenon. Originating in the United States in the early 1950s with the synthesis of black rhythm-and-blues and white country-and-western music, the genre is less than four decades old. Although the quantity of written material amassed on the subject is impressive for such a young form, rock-and-roll literature is still in the developmental stages.

The large quantity of writing on rock-and-roll can be attributed to the fact that the style has gained wide appeal among international audiences as a form of popular entertainment. However, the status of rock-and-roll as a popular entertainment form, as opposed to a classical or "serious" art form, is also responsible for limiting the type of writing on the subject, for the most part, to journalistic treatments rather than scholarly studies. Classical art forms tend to conform to particular aesthetic codes and are slow to absorb radical alteration of structure or content. In contrast, rock-and-roll has welcomed spontaneity, experimentation, and change from its very inception. The rebellious nature of the genre, together with its relative newness as a distinct expressive form, has insulated it from serious scholarly study.

New York underground rock and punk rock, two subgenres of rock-and-roll, pose even greater problems in terms of historical documentation and scholarly study. Central to the punk philosophy is the anthem "no future" (taken from lyrics of "God Save the Queen" 1976, a song by the Sex Pistols—most famous of the punk-rock bands). This pessimistic attitude toward the future is partially responsible for a lack of interest within punk culture in documenting the history of the movement. Much of the primary material generated by punk culture was intentionally ephemeral. Marian Kester, in *Streetart,* coauthored with Peter Belsito and Bob Davis, explains that punk paraphernalia was "designed to be trash . . . throwaway art" (1981, 9). Therefore many fanzines (small publications which catered to punk-rock fans) were unnumbered, undated, and anonymously written. Small nightclubs which catered to underground-rock and punk-rock performances were by and large uninterested in or unaware of any role they may have been playing in a historic movement. They usually kept records of their activities for only a few weeks, if at all. For these reasons the historian must rely on oral history to a large degree in an investigation of this period. Here again problems arise because of the difficulty in finding punk rockers who are willing to discuss their activities during this period. Many people who figured prominently in the development of punk style are unwilling to grant interviews concerning their participation in, and/or influence on, the movement for a variety of personal and professional reasons. Some (including Lou Reed, John Cale, David Bowie, and Johnny Rotten) are primarily interested in their current work and refused to be interviewed concerning the punk movement.

The difficulties of researching punk are further complicated by the fact that punk rock developed specific aesthetic codes in order to rebel against, and make itself inaccessible to, the cultural mainstream. The process of documenting the particulars of this aesthetic and subjecting them to scholarly analysis renders the punk code accessible to outsiders—thereby subverting its rebellious nature. In point of fact, few of the punk rockers I was able to contact were willing to submit their work to what they considered to be a study antithetical to their philosophy.

The nature of rock-and-roll literature also presents problems in terms of scholarly research. Articles in the popular press (newspapers, magazines, etc.) made nonpractitioners aware of the existence of the punk movement but made little attempt to understand the causes or analyze the content of punk. The effect of mainstream media exposure was to frighten and alienate the general public and afford the punks a sinister notoriety which underscored and amplified their rebellious intentions. These articles, while interesting in themselves—both as an indication of the impact punk was having on the public consciousness at that time and as a barometer of public feeling towards the punk phenomenon—are of limited use to the serious scholar.

Articles in trade rock-and-roll newspapers (*Rolling Stone, Melody Maker, Sounds,* etc.) provide a deeper insight and some analysis of the underlying social forces at work in the punk movement but are still basically journalistic treatments of the subject. These articles generally consist of subjective critiques of bands and performances. They are rarely footnoted and seldom documented in more than a perfunctory manner.

There are no serious scholarly journals dedicated to rock-and-roll music. Occasionally an article on rock-and-roll music will appear in an academic publication. Articles which deal specifically with punk rock, such as W. T. Lahmon's "Dadapunk" in *Bennington Review* (1980, 39), while highly informative, are extremely rare.

Rock-and-roll histories such as *The Rolling Stone Illustrated History of Rock & Roll* (Miller, ed. 1980), *The Rock and Roll Story* (Brown 1983), and *Twenty-Five Years of Rock 'n' Roll Style* (Stewart, ed. 1982) are useful in placing punk rock in an historical perspective. Because the scope of rock history covers a wide range of topics, from the pre–Elvis Presley era of rock (late 1940s and often earlier) up to and including bands popular today, they must necessarily treat the punk movement in a superficial manner.

To date, several books have been published which deal specifically with punk rock. They include: *Punk* (Anscombe and Blair 1978); *Primal Punk* (Bladow and Ivins 1982); *Punk Rock* (Boston 1978); *The Boy Looked at Johnny* (Burchill and Parsons 1978); *1988: The New Wave Punk Rock Explosion* (Coon 1977); and *New Wave Explosion* (Palmer 1981). These books, while offering valuable collections of photographs, interviews, and informative editorials written by punk-rock fans, are subjective documentations of the punk movement and, as is the case with other printed matter on the subject, are not documented in a manner which allows extensive verification.

Because a serious study of punk rock and the evolution of its style has not previously been undertaken, I have referred to scholarly studies in related areas for theoretical grounding and research models. The most helpful of these include *The Sociology of Youth Culture and Youth Subcultures* (Brake 1980) and *Subculture: The Meaning of Style* (Hebdige 1979).

Over the past eight years, I have worked extensively in New York City and London. In the course of my research, I have visited as many of the gathering places and performance venues of the punk-rock movement as possible. I have interviewed key figures; amassed primary data (fanzines, posters, photographs, newsclippings, etc.) from the personal collections of punk-rock fans; collected audio and video recordings of punk-rock performances; and acquired sheet music in the rare instances when it was available.

Because of the transitory nature of punk rock, primary sources are fast disappearing. It is therefore imperative that this research and data be compiled now, as it will only become more difficult to gather in the future.

The classic punk style crystallized in England in 1976. British bands developed a new and distinct sound and together with their fans created an ambiance for their music that soon grew into a dynamic and unique subculture. Their new style, though deeply influenced by the rebellious nature of New York–based bands, was different. In the mid-1970s, Great Britain was suffering from one of the highest unemployment rates the country had seen since World War II, and a steadily rising cost of living exacerbated a mood of unrest and discontent among working class people forced to struggle for the basic necessities of existence. For the large number of people on welfare—or "the dole," as it is known in Great Britain—especially young people, the outlook for bettering their lot in life seemed bleak. In this atmosphere, when the English were exposed to the seminal punk-rock influences of the New York scene, the irony, pessimism, and amateur style of the music took on overt social and political implications, and British punk became as self-consciously proletarian as it was aesthetic.

In order to distinguish between the distinct American and British styles, the following terms will be used here; "underground rock" will refer to the experimental rock music which developed in New York City from 1965 to 1975. "Punk rock" refers to the British musical style in evidence between 1975 and 1979 as epitomized by the music of the London–based band the Sex Pistols. As the evolution of the punk style is discussed, the differences between these two trends and their relationships to one another will become apparent.

The study of the evolution of punk style begins in New York with Lou Reed and the Velvet Underground. I will examine their work in terms of how it predicted the punk style: the choice of subject matter commonly deemed offensive to the middle class (drugs, deviant sex, etc.), the deliberately amateurish quality of the music, and the generally pessimistic attitude towards the future. This antisocial, nonconformist approach resulted in an uncommercial product which thrived on a cult following rather than a broad popular appeal. Andy Warhol's conncections with the Velvet Underground will be discussed in this context, particularly in relation to the *Exploding Plastic Inevitable.*

I follow the progression from underground rock to glitter rock, concentrating on the work of the New York Dolls and David Bowie. These artists, with their emphasis on ambiguous sexuality and sexual role playing opened up "questions of sexual identity which had previously been repressed, ignored, or merely hinted at in rock and youth culture" (Hebdige 1979, 61). Bowie's music, though not overtly political or representative of any particular countercultural movement, is germane to the punk issue because of its message of escapism. His adoption of various stage personalities implied not only that it was acceptable to be whomever or whatever one wished to be, but that the cultural taboos which inhibit unusual, outrageous, or antisocial behavior can and should be ignored. Not everyone, however, was comfortable with male rock heros in high heels and dresses. The punk aesthetic, with its "working-classness, scruffiness, and earthiness" can be said to be an antithetical reaction to the "extreme foppishness, insipient elitism, and morbid pretentions to art and intellect" of the purveyors of glitter rock (ibid.).

In surveying the CBGB scene in New York, including the work of Television, Patti Smith, and the Ramones, I explore the most immediate precursors of the punk movement in England. Malcolm McLaren's influence is investigated, as he represents a direct link between the New York underground-rock movement and the punk style in Great Britain.

In the chapter on British punk and the Sex Pistols, I describe the punk phenomenon at the peak of its development. The raw, harsh, unrestrained nature of the music is seen as an organic outgrowth of the New York underground-rock movement,[1] and yet qualitatively different. Special attention is paid to the clothing, personal adornment, dance style, and behavioral attitudes exhibited by the practitioners of the punk aesthetic. In addition, the class differences between the British punks and their American counterparts are examined. The underground-rock movement consisted primarily of middle-class youths rejecting middle-class values. In Britain, punk generally represented working-class youths reacting to the bourgeois status quo.⟩

⟨In the final chapter I discuss fanzines—publications produced by punks for their peers. In style, content, graphics, and overall tone of writing, the fanzines present a mirror image of the punk lifestyle. Representative examples of fanzines will be examined in terms of their relationship to punk culture. Among the few primary sources of written material concerning punk rock, the fanzines are invaluable in affording the reader an insider's view of the punk phenomenon.⟩

It would be impossible in a work of this scope to mention every influence that led to the development of the punk phenomenon. Among the major figures outside the parameters of this work, but who nevertheless figured prominently as precursors of the punk movement, are Elvis Presley, the Rolling Stones, the MC5, Alice Cooper, and Iggy Pop and the Stooges. It would take a work of encyclopedic proportions to tie in every facet of rock culture that had an influence on punk. Moreover, in focusing on the work of the Sex Pistols, the archetypal punk band, I am able to illustrate the most visible and characteristic elements of the punk idiom. Unfortunately, limitations of time and space require that I ignore literally hundreds of punk bands who, each in their own way, contributed to the punk movement. Likewise, the social, economic, and political ramifications of punk are too far-reaching to treat exhaustively in a work of this nature. Obviously there is room for more scholarly research in these areas. The people on whom I have chosen to concentrate have had the most immediate influence on the development of punk. A direct line can be drawn from the work of Lou Reed, through the glitter rock of David Bowie and the New York Dolls, to the CBGB scene, and from there to British punk rock. This study concentrates on the aesthetic influences of these figures on the development of punk style. I establish this relationship, and document it as thoroughly as possible.

The Bobst Library, New York University; the Mid-Manhattan Library, New York Public Library; the Music Library, New York Public Library; the Library of Congress; and the British Museum have been invaluable sources of printed material in the course of my research. The Recording Industry Association of America; the American Society of Composers, Authors, and Publishers (ASCAP); Mercury Records; Oakfield Avenue Music, Limited; Polygram Records; Carl Fischer, Inc.; and Virgin Records have also been helpful in locating sheet music and artist biographies, and in providing data on recording industry policies.

I am also grateful to Hilly Kristal, owner of CBGB, Peter Jordan, former member of the New York Dolls, and John Holmstrom, editor of *Punk* magazine, for their continuing interest in this project, including extensive personal interviews and assistance in locating rare primary data on underground-rock and punk-rock music. I am also indebted to Bob Gruen, Gerard Malanga, and Mark Ivins for allowing me access to their personal photo archives.

I would like to thank Greg Presley, Assistant Professor of Music, Florida State University for his assistance in analyzing musical scores and audio recordings; and Mark Striffler, Entertainment Booking Agent, Florida State University for his help in locating and interviewing key figures in the rock music industry, and for his patient instruction in music industry policies.

I wish to express my deep appreciation to Dr. Nancy Smith Fichter, Chair, Department of Dance, Florida State University, Dr. Jerry Draper, Dean, School of Visual Arts, Florida State University, Dr. Sally R. Sommer, Gregory O'Hara, and Thomas Austin for their continuing advice and moral support; Charles O'Hara for his skilful and patient editing of the text, as well as his invaluable contributions to the work; and my parents, Billie and J. D. Henry, for their love, faith, and encouragement.

Introduction

The politics and aesthetics of punk rock, while spontaneous and distinct in themselves, contain many similarities to the politics and aesthetics of certain movements in the historical avant-garde of the twentieth century. Punk rock, like the avant-garde, is revolutionary. It is a reaction against established theories and techniques of art, as well as against the society which produces them. It prizes the artist as revolutionary, and asserts a philosophy which it considers to be a more pertinent view of the world than that reflected by traditional values. It also creates an artist's world—a social stratum specifically oriented toward the arts. The term "avant-garde," meaning literally the "advance guard," is comparable to the punk idea of the "new wave." Both describe active forces at the edge of change.

In striving to build an aesthetic that they felt was meaningful to their lives, punks used many of the same revolutionary tactics employed by members of early avant-garde movements: unusual fashions; the blurring of boundaries between art and everyday life; juxtapositions of seemingly disparate objects and behaviors; intentional provocation of the audience; use of untrained performers; and drastic reorganization (or disorganization) of accepted performative styles and procedures.

The punk scene in England in the late 1970s was the real core of the punk movement—that is where the style first crystallized and became popular. Members of the movement were basically lower-class white youths who were hit hard by Britain's economic situation. They felt that they had "no future" (one of the slogans which became synonymous with the punk world view), and that their lives had been predestined by a society run by people with unfair advantages (i.e., money and political power). When they finished high school, if they did, they either couldn't find work or were doomed to jobs which they found unbearably boring, and which offered no creative challenge and very little pay. Like members of earlier avant-garde movements they were antibourgeois and anticapitalist.

In order to protest their situation, the punks presented themselves as society's garbage, as if to say, "We are your children, what do you think of your creation?" Punk fashion drew on cultural sore points such as sadomasochism. Bondage wear, chains, heavy leathers, and other S&M paraphernalia were popular, as well as new variations on the theme, including razor-blade jewelry and safety pins worn through flesh. The idea was to look as horrifyingly repugnant as possible. Sex was meant to horrify rather than to entice.

Fascism, as an element of fashion, was another shock tactic. Nazi regalia became quite popular, though they seem to have been used to remind society of the atrocities it permits, rather than as a symbol of a thriving fascist philosophy. To my knowledge there were no punks in the ranks of the National Front.

Punk fashion was antifashion—anything that was ugly or offensive to the general public; anything "unnatural": multicolored hair spiked up with Vaseline; the ragged haircut; exaggerated make-up—the 1940s horror movie look. Vivienne Westwood, a London clothing designer who was responsible for creating much of the punk aesthetic, became known for what Dike Blair calls her "manifesto":

> Vivienne Westwood . . . sloganizes her designs as "Clothes for Heros," and says that to wear them is to express an attitude and a commitment—and you have to be brave to wear her clothes. You make a spectacle of yourself on the street, and a spectacle is a show of force inviting opposition: the irony of bondage wear. . . . However, clothes can often express ideas better than words. They can be as subversive a weapon as a book, poster or pamphlet: the person sitting next to you on the bus in an "Anarchy in the U.K." T-shirt has an immediate impact. (Blair 1978, 62)

The punks used fashion as a revolutionary tool in much the same way the Russian futurists did. Futurism was a movement founded in 1909 by Filippo Marinetti with his "Foundation and Manifesto of Futurism," published in the large-circulation Paris daily *Le Figaro*. Like other movements in the historical avant-garde, it was an interdisciplinary movement which included visual art, literature, and performance. It was dedicated to the rejection of traditional art forms, non-naturalist expression, and audience involvement. The Russian futurists "took their futurism to the public: they walked the streets in outrageous attire; their faces painted, sporting top hats, velvet jackets, earrings, and radishes or spoons in their buttonholes" (Goldberg 1979, 22). The punks, who wanted to take their social sentiments to the streets, walked the King's Road in London sporting chains, dog collars, multicolored hair, and horror-movie-style make-up with similarly disturbing effects on the public.

Among the punk population much exchange of information took place through street-level distribution of small publications called "fanzines." Besides providing information about events and performances, and providing an alternative to mainstream criticism, these fanzines included a variety of what Dick

Hebdige, in his book *Subculture: The Meaning of Style*, refers to as manifestoes. In describing one such item he writes:

> *Sniffin' Glue*, the first fanzine and the one which achieved the highest circulation, contained perhaps the single most inspired item of propaganda produced by the subculture—the definitive statement of punk's do-it-yourself philosophy—a diagram showing three finger positions on the neck of a guitar over the caption: "Here's one chord, here's two more, now form your own band." (Hebdige 1979, 112)

In addition to providing a network of philosophical exchange within the punk population, the fanzines contributed another important element: the establishment of a graphic aesthetic. Like punk fashion, punk art was low-budget and easily accessible. It was antiglossy: handwritten, photocopied, black-and-white (high contrast), and collage. It was subversive by its very appearance.

Punk collage echoed the juxtaposing of disparate elements in punk fashion. This juxtaposing of seemingly unrelated or disproportionate objects is also a well-known aspect of dada and surrealism. Dada, generally placed between 1916 and 1922, gained notoriety in France shortly after World War I for vigorously rejecting all previously existing social and aesthetic values. It preached nonsense and anti-art and used parody and off-color humor to antagonize its audiences. Marcel Duchamp, a leading figure in dada, became famous for his "readymades," which he created by simply putting his signature on objects such as urinals, bottle racks, and snow shovels and exhibiting them as works of art. Another dadaist, Hans Arp, invented a kind of collage in which he dropped bits of colored paper onto a larger sheet to create works of art that incorporated chance relationships.

Surrealism, founded in 1924 by a group of Duchamp's colleagues, was interested in the nonrational, nonlogical[1] mind rather than the rational, logical one. Surrealism did not project the canceling-out of one thing by another as dada did, but rather allowed the coexistence of separate, incongruous realities. It sought to express the workings of the subconscious mind, particularly as manifested by dreams, and "untranslated" by the conscious, analytical mind. The landscapes (or "dreamscapes") of Salvador Dali are good examples.

The punk collages varied in their attitudes from the absurdity of dada to the "piercing through of another reality" of surrealism.[2] Not all punk collage fits into the categorie~ of dadaism or surrealism, but despite the varying styles involved, they all have one thing in common: they put familiar objects into unfamiliar relationships, changing meaning by shifting context.

Punk performance, like punk fashion and art, is subversive. It is an assault on the senses. Though it underwent considerable refinement, in the early days (mid-1970s) performances took place in small, crowded, low-budget spaces in notoriously rough neighborhoods. Performers, for the most part, had little or no technical training and possessed only very cheap and unsophisticated equipment. The decibel level was brutally high, and the attitudes of both performers and audience members were aggressive and often verged on violence. As part of the punk policy of provocation, performers were known to include in their performances behavior such as vomiting on stage, spitting at the audience, and displaying wounds which were the result of self-mutilation—having cut and bruised themselves with objects such as broken bottles, fish hooks, and knives. The audience's role often included throwing "permanently" affixed seating, beer bottles, glasses, and anything else that made itself available at the performers. Performer-audience confrontation was also an element of futurist and dadaist performances: the audience's riotious response to the profance language and arrogant attitude of the performers in Alfred Jarry's *Ubu Roi* (as well as numerous other futurist performances) is well known, as is the protest which met Richard Huelsenbeck's provocative performances in Berlin in which he praised war, attacked expressionism, and insulted the audience.

Members of the punk movement have often referred to themselves as "neo-dada." For example, in their book *Punk,* advertised as an inside view of the scene, the authors write: "It was a tough, aggressive medium. The graffiti, collage, and fashion, all elements of punk, have a neo-dada flavor" (Blair et al. 1978, 102). Concerts have also been advertised as "neo-dada" performances. Punks have also felt an alliance with the futurist movement. Belsito, Davis, and Kester, for example, include the following dedication in their book *Street Art:*

> This book is dedicated to Filippo Marinetti (1876–1944), poet and visionary of the Futurist movement, who wrote:
>
> "We want to sing the love of danger, the habit of danger, and of temerity."
>
> "There is no more beauty except in struggle. No masterpiece without an aggressive character." (Belsito, Davis, and Kester 1981, 2)

Though none of these writers or artists elaborate on the connection between punk and the avant-garde, certain relationships are clear. The attitudes of revolution and confrontation are two common denominators. The use of "raw" material—the lack of technical training or the transcendence of it—is another. The solicitation of nonactors for Mayakovsky's *Victory over the Sun,* for instance, is comparable to Duchamp's readymades, and punk's Johnny Rotten, who was selected as lead singer for the Sex Pistols because of his aggressive looks rather than his ability to sing. The idea of intellectual expertise rather than technical expertise runs through all three movements—the expertise lies in the originality of ideas rather than in technical training.

Although the punks seemed, with their masochistic tendencies, to be against everything, even themselves—like the dadaists who were against everything, including dada—this was not really the case. Masochism was a shock tactic used, along with other subversive elements of punk, to make a point. The punks were for showing the public what they thought of society; they were for anarchy; they were for developing a new style of music with which they could identify; and they were for making that music accessible—through independent record labels, fanzines, and performances—to their peers and eventually to the general public. This was very different from the dada attitude of the destruction of logic. Punk behavior was not alogical—it was a very consistent and systematic method of expressing feelings about specific social and aesthetic issues.

In its actual staging, punk performance bears a strong resemblance to expressionist performance. Expressionism was a movement originating in Europe before World War I which asserted the expression of the inner, emotional experience of a person rather than the expression of realistic appearances. As opposed to the contemplative, fragile, and dreamlike nature of symbolist performance, punk, like expressionism, is assertive, assaultive, and very much here-and-now. Also like expressionism, it seeks to invoke an empathetic response in the observer through sensory attack and emotional overload. The scream, emblematic of the expressionist movement, is also a recurring motif in punk—both in the delivery of lyrics and in graphic art.

Punk also invokes an empathetic response through body language. Like expressionism, it presents a convulsive and hyperactive figure. Exaggerated make-up also contributes to empathetic response—horror-movie-style make-up for example, popular among punks, and the nerves painted on the bodies of the performers in Kokoschka's *Murderer, the Women's Hope,* both evoke strong emotional responses in the viewer. In *The Cabinet of Dr. Caligari,* a noted expressionist film by Robert Weine, Carl Mayer, and Hans Janowitz, the characters display both the exaggerated make-up and the convulsive, hyperactive figure to produce a visual and emotional impact strikingly similar to punk. The intense decibel level, and close proximity of audience and performers (important aspects of punk performance) also add to the intensity—physical and emotional empathy crowding out immediate intellectual response.

The interest in an interdisciplinary approach to art—an important feature of the avant-garde—has greatly influenced punk rock. According to Blair:

Performance artists finally found an audience. The first punk bands in New York used to play the Mercer Arts Center; in Toronto, Cleveland, and San Francisco, art schools added musicians and audiences to the local scenes. Patti Smith and Tom Verlaine were on the poetry circuit before settling on rock 'n' roll. Talking Heads met in art school, Amos Poe mixes punk and film, there's lots of video, and everybody's got cameras—punk is so photogenic. (Blair et al. 1978, 102)

The difference, however, between the interdisciplinary approach of the avant-garde and that of punk is that the avant-garde is usually interested in transcending boundaries between the arts from the very inception of a movement; while punk, like other rock-and-roll movements, is musically oriented. Punk style influenced other arts, not through a conscious effort to instigate an interdisciplinary artistic movement, but by way of artists such as Laurie Anderson and Karole Armitage, who were interested in drawing on the punk aesthetic for primary material in much the same way the futurists drew on circus and variety theatre.

Although, as we have seen, punk shares many of its revolutionary tactics with the avant-garde and expresses a conscious alliance with it, the relationship between the two is debatable. While the primary concern of the avant-garde is artistic rebellion, the primary concern of punk, like other youth subcultures (teds, mods, greasers, hippies, etc.) is social rebellion. Though the two concerns are closely intertwined and often inseparable, it is clear that the avant-garde is most self-consciously artistic, while punk is most self-consciously proletariat.

Punk rock has been a significant factor in shaping Western aesthetic trends since the mid-1970s. It has influenced not only the evolution of performing arts but also of fashion, graphic arts, literature, film, and popular entertainment. Rebelling against the conservative social, political, and aesthetic climate of the 1970s, practioners of punk rock sought to create a mode of expression which reflected the views of a new generation of urban performers. Originating as an affront to the general public, punk was characterized by aggressive antisocial behavior and an artistic sensibility emphasizing dissonance.

The development of punk rock was precipitated by a cultural exchange between the United States and Great Britain. The classic punk style had its roots in American popular entertainment—most notably the New York City nightclub scene. Beginning in 1965 and continuing through the 1970s, New York bands such as the Velvet Underground, the New York Dolls, and the Ramones produced a new kind of music which was self-consciously "streetwise" and pessimistic about the future. The unrelenting beat, abrasive sound, and amateur style of this new music set it apart from the more optimistic world view and technical polish of mainstream rock. A strong connection with the New York City avant-garde further distinguished it from the commercial elements of mainstream culture. For example, Andy Warhol worked with the Velvet Underground to create the *Exploding Plastic Inevitable,* Warhol's travelling mixed-media circus of 1966–67. The *Exploding Plastic Inevitable* broke new ground in establishing the creative possibilities of rock-and-roll as an artistic theatrical performance.

Susan Sontag points out in her essay "Notes on Camp" that "many things in the world have never been named; and many things, even if they have been named, have never been described" (1966, 275). "Punk," as in "punk rock" and "punk culture," is such a phenomenon. The term has never been clearly defined. It has been used in reference to a great variety of people and performances spanning (so far) a fifteen-year period. Though "punk" did not become a generic term used in reference to a certain type of rock-and-roll music and the youth subculture associated with it until the emergence of the punk scene in Britain in 1975, it has also been used, mainly in retrospect, to describe noncommercial rock music of the early 1970s as well as highly commercial rock music of the early 1980s. In addition, "punk" has sometimes been used synonymously with other terms such as "underground rock" (Wolcott, August 1975, 6), "new wave" (Robbins 1985, 320; Miller 1976, 423; Jordan 1986, interview), "new music" (Blackwood 1986, interview; Kristal 1986, interview), "street rock" (Kristal 1986, interview), "power pop" (Bladow and Ivins 1982, 3), "avant-punk" (Christgau, October 1977, 57), and "hardcore" (Belsito and Davis 1983, 1).[3] This lack of precision with which the term "punk" has been used has been responsible for a widespread misunderstanding of the evolution of punk rock, as well as confusion concerning its specific characteristics.

The origins of the word "punk" are obscure. It first appeared in the English language as a synonym for prostitute. The 1971 edition of *The Oxford English Dictionary* refers to its use by Shakespeare in 1603 in his comedy *Measure for Measure:* "She may be a Puncke, for many of them are neither Maid, Widow, nor Wife." *The Oxford English Dictionary* also makes reference to Thomas Middleton, who in 1607 emphasized the singularly derogatory nature of the word: "I may grace her with the name of Curtizan, a Backslider, a Prostitution, or such a Toy, but when all comes to al tis but a plaine Pung" (1971). Over the years the word gradually came to be used to describe a male homosexual or catamite. Though prostitute and homosexual are still dictionary definitions of the word "punk," in the twentieth century it has taken on new meanings, and the sexual connotations are for the most part archaic. *Funk and Wagnalls New Standard Dictionary of the English Language* defines "punk" as:

> n. 1. Wood decayed as through the actions of some fungus; vegetable tinder; touchwood: hence (slang, chiefly U.S.) any worthless object or empty talk. 2. A preparation that will smoulder without flame; amadou; especially a composition made into sticks and used to touch off fireworks, etc. (1966)

Further definitions include its use to mean a blow or punch with a closed fist. "Punk" can also refer to a young gangster, a hoodlum, or merely a person who is regarded as inexperienced. The most common use of the word, according to Funk and Wagnalls, is as a slang term: "Of no use whatever: worthless; applied figuratively as a term of derision."

While these dictionary definitions are interesting and instructive, they are by no means the last word on the subject. In a living language, words in common usage often outgrow their meanings faster than dictionaries can keep up with them. Recently "punk" has acquired new connotations, being used to describe the phenomenon known as "punk rock." Although, as already mentioned, the term "punk rock" has yet to be carefully and clearly defined, the underlying implications of the amateur, the hoodlum, the useless element in society, together with the idea of volatility, make the term a logical and emotionally loaded choice as a reference to stylistic phenomena at the radical end of the rock-and-roll continuum.

In July 1975, Richard Mortifoglio, in a *Village Voice* review of the New York–based band Television, described the group as having "allegiances with punk rock" (7 July 1977, 96). Though Mortifoglio does not explain his use of the term, he notes that the artistic sensibility of the band "has sprung up in the precious soil between the cracks in the concrete," inferring that the group's style tended towards independence from the commercial mainstream.

In New York City in January 1976, a magazine appeared called *Punk,* which was centered around a series of concerts given at a small club named CBGB & OMFUG in Manhattan's East Village. CBGB opened its doors in March 1974. It quickly became popular with aspiring young musicians because it offered them a venue for the performance of original material outside the parameters of mainstream rock-and-roll. Rebellious in nature, the CBGB scene and its association with the term "punk" through *Punk* magazine were the first steps in establishing the term "punk rock" as a description of a particular experimental rock-and-roll movement.

When Lou Reed and John Cale founded the Velvet Underground in 1965, a series of events was set in motion that would change the direction of rock music and serve as a catalyst for the development of punk rock. Lou Reed is the prototype of the true punk rocker. A gifted poet, musician, and performer, he not only personified all the qualities and nuances of style now associated with the word punk, but, in effect, he almost singlehandedly invented the musical genre that later developed into the classical punk-rock style. He was a revelation and an inspiration to scores of performers who would follow in his footsteps.

1

Lou Reed, the Velvet Underground, and the *Exploding Plastic Inevitable*

In 1965 in New York City, Lou Reed and John Cale founded the Velvet Underground, a rock-and-roll band which greatly influenced the direction of popular music in the late 1960s and early 1970s. The Velvet Underground was a catalyst for a series of events that eventually led to the development of punk rock.

Reed, a pianist, lyricist, and guitarist, played professionally in rock bands following his years in college. Raised in a middle-class Brooklyn family, he attended Syracuse University from 1960 to 1964, where he studied journalism and poetry with the late Delmore Schwartz (to whom he dedicated "European Son" (1967) on the first Velvet Underground album *The Velvet Underground and Nico*). He also played in two local Syracuse bands: L.A. and the Eldorados.

In 1964, after leaving Syracuse, Reed worked as a studio musician and songwriter for Pickwick City Records in New York City. Pickwick, in operation from 1953 to 1982, was a budget record company which marketed inexpensive forty-five and thirty-three r.p.m. records. Pickwick specialized in records which closely resembled best-selling popular releases, both in musical style and record cover design. All Pickwick records were written and recorded by the company's studio musicians. These musicians performed under a variety of names, in accordance with the band or type of band which they emulated. According to Mike West, in his book *The Velvet Underground and Lou Reed,* Pickwick specialized in "whole albums of Mock Merseybeat[1] and Phoney Folk to satisfy the undiscerning and fool the few" (1982, 6). Reed explained in a 1972 *Rolling Stone* interview with Mick Rock: "They'd put me in a room and say 'We want ten hot rod songs and ten surfin' songs,' and I would write them" (1972, 14).

Pickwick recorded several of Reed's songs. Among these early releases, recorded by the Beachnuts, the Roughnecks, and the Primitives—the studio bands with whom Reed played at Pickwick—were "Sneaky Pete" (1964), "The Ostrich" (1964), "Cycle Annie" (1965), and "You're Driving Me Insane" (1965). The lyrical content of several of these songs departed from the common romantic themes of 1960s popular music. For example, "The Ostrich," a spoof on dance-craze singles popular at the time, contained the dance instructions, "You put your head on the floor and have someone step on it." However, these songs were not nearly as shocking as Reed's subsequent recordings of "Heroin" (1966) and "Venus in Furs" (1966). Pickwick refused to record these songs because of their references to drugs and sadomasochism, and it was not until the formation of the Velvet Underground in 1966 that they were produced. From these recordings we see the full development of Reed's streetwise, sardonic style for which he would later become famous.

In 1964, while still working for Pickwick records, Reed met John Cale, a classically trained violist, pianist, singer, and composer from Wales. Cale trained at London University's Goldsmiths' College from 1960 to 1963 and also studied with British composer Humphrey Searle. He came to the United States in 1963 under the auspices of a Leonard Bernstein fellowship to study with Aaron Copland at the Eastman Conservatory at Tanglewood in Lenox, Massachusetts. In 1964, Cale moved to New York City and began working with John Cage and LeMonte Young, with whom he founded the Dream Syndicate. According to Victor Bockris and Gerard Malanga, in their history of the Velvet Underground, *Uptight: The Velvet Underground Story:*

> The members of The Dream Syndicate, motivated by a scientific and mystical fascination with sound, spent long hours in rehearsals learning to provide sustained meditative drones and chants. This rigorous style served to discipline John and developed his knowledge of the just intonation system. He also learned to use his viola in a new amplified way which would lead to the powerful droning effect that is so strong in the first two Velvet Underground records. (1983, 13)

Cale was interested in extending the vocabulary of rock-and-roll beyond the standard components of 4/4 beat and guitar/bass/drums/keyboard instrumental make-up. His custom-electrified viola equipped with guitar strings and his carefully structured "noise" arrangements were essential in setting apart the musical style of the Velvet Underground from mainstream popular music trends.

Reed and Cale formed a band called the Falling Spikes in the fall of 1965. They worked with Sterling Morrison, a guitarist Reed had met at Syracuse, and drummer/artist Walter DeMaria. When DeMaria left the band, he was replaced by Angus MacLise, a Scottish drummer and poet who worked as percussionist for LeMonte Young. The group was also known briefly as the Warlocks before settling on the name Velvet Underground in November of 1965. According to Reed (*Rock* 1972, 13) and others (Malanga 1986, interview) the Velvet Underground took its name from a novel dealing with sadomasochism written by Michael Leigh in 1963.

By November 1965 the Velvet Underground consisted of Reed (vocals, guitar, keyboards), Cale (bass, keyboards, viola), Sterling Morrison (guitar), and Maureen Tucker (drums). Although each band member made an important contribution to the group's overall sound and style, Reed was the most significant creative force behind it. Most of the Velvet Underground's original material was written by Reed,[2] who also served as lead singer. His lyrical content, musical structure, and stage performance made him the most important member of the band. Under his guidance and direction the Velvet Underground developed a sound and a style that incorporated many elements which later became associated with punk. The aesthetic sensibility of the punk rock movement of the 1970s can be traced directly to the work Reed was doing at this time.

Reed's lyrical content foreshadowed punk style in its deliberate departure from popular musical trends. It focused on subject matter deemed inappropriate by the general public. The lyrics of "Heroin" and "Venus in Furs" exemplify Reed's controversial lyrical content. Dealing graphically with heroin use and sadomasochism, the attitudes expressed in these songs ran directly counter to the more optimistic and romantic "boy-meets-girl" themes so popular in mid-1960s rock-and-roll. Songs like "I'm a Believer" by the Monkees, "We Can Work It Out" by the Beatles, "You're My Soul and Inspiration" by the Righteous Brothers, and "Cherish" by the Association were number one hit songs in the 1966 *Billboard* ratings.[3] To appreciate the difference, let us first examine the lyrics to "Heroin":

Heroin

I don't know just where I'm going
But I'm gonna try for the kingdom if I can
'Cause it makes me feel like I'm a man
When I put the spike into my vein
Then I tell you things aren't quite the same
When I'm rushing on my run
And I feel just like Jesus' son
And I guess I just don't know
And I guess that I just don't know

I have made a very big decision
I'm going to try to nullify my life
'Cause when the blood begins to flow
When it shoots up the dropper's neck
When I'm closing in on death
You can't help me, not you guys
Or all you silly girls with your sweet talk
You can all go take a walk
And I guess that I just don't know
And I guess that I just don't know

I wish that I was born a thousand years ago
I wish that I'd sailed the darkened seas
On a great big clipper ship
Going from this land here to that
I put on a sailor's suit and cap
Away from the big city
Where a man cannot be free
Of all the evils in this town
And of himself and those around
And I guess that I just don't know
And I guess that I just don't know

Heroin
Gonna be the death of me
Heroin
It's my wife and its my life
Because a mainer to my vein
Leads to a center in my head
And then I'm better off than dead
When the smack begins to flow
Then I really don't care any more
About all you jim-jims in this town
And everybody putting everybody else down
And all the politicians making crazy sounds
And all the dead bodies piled up in mounds
But while that heroin is in my blood
And that blood is in my head
Thank God I'm as good as dead
Thank God that I'm not aware
And thank God that I just don't care
And I guess that I just don't know
And I guess that I just don't know

The title itself is disturbing. Heroin evokes images that are disturbing, offensive, and frightening to middle-class sensibilities. These lyrics certainly do not glamorize the use of drugs except in the sense that self-destruction and death might seem glamorous to social misfits. According to Sterling Morrison, "It should be pointed out that when Reed sings he's only glamorizing heroin for people who want to die" (Bockris and Malanga 1983, 74). In fact, it is easy to interpret the song as having an antidrug message. If anything, Reed deals with the problem in a straightforward manner, exposing drug addiction as a basically empty, futile, and ultimately painful form of escapism. While he no doubt appreciated the shock value of drug abuse as subject matter for a song, particularly as a symbolic affront to middle-class values, his songs should not be construed as an endorsement of the use of drugs by others. "Heroin" expresses pessimism about the self, the future, and society. It clearly anticipates the punk anthems "No Future" and "I Don't Care," which became popular in punk culture in the late 1970s.

"Venus in Furs" deals with another cultural taboo: sadomasochism. Like "Heroin," "Venus in Furs" foreshadowed punk lyrical content in its inclusion of subject matter unacceptable to mainstream sensibilities.

Venus in Furs

Shiny shiny shiny boots of leather
Whiplash girlchild, in the dark
Comes in bells your servant don't forsake him
Strike dear mistress and cure his heart

Chorus:
I am tired, I am weary
I could sleep four thousand years
A thousand dreams that would awake me
Different colors made of tears

Downy sins of streetlight fancies
Chase the costumes she must wear
Ermine furs adorn imperious,
Severin, Severin, awaits you there
(Chorus repeat)

Kiss the boot of shiny, shiny leather
Shiny, shiny leather in the dark
Tongue the thongs, the belt that does await you
Strike dear mistress and cure his heart
(Chorus repeat)

Severin, Severin, speak so slightly
Severin down on your bended knees
Taste the whip, in love not given lightly
Severin taste the whip now bleed for me
(Chorus repeat)

Shiny, shiny shiny boots of leather
Whiplash girlchild in the dark
Severin, your servant, comes in bells, please don't forsake him
Strike dear mistress and cure his heart

The title of "Venus in Furs" is taken from the title of a novel by Leopold von Sacher-Masoch, for whom masochism is named. The song vividly depicts a sadomasochistic relationship. This is a far cry from images of romantic love evoked in the Hot 100 hit songs of 1966, or even 1986. Reed evokes the forbidden, dangerous aspects of life and love. James Wolcott, music critic for the *Village Voice,* discussed the lyrical content of the Velvet Underground's songs in his article "The Rise of Punk Rock":

> Even their most beautiful love songs ("Pale Blue Eyes," "I'll Be Your Mirror") were about the distances between people—about the inability to penetrate the mystery of the other. The drug they sang about was not a vision-inducing agent like acid, or a partytime pass-it-around substance like pot, but the drug that most completely isolates one from others: heroin. The Velvet's music was about nihilism, the nihilism of the street. (Wolcott 1976, 87)

According to John Pareles and Patricia Romanowski, in *The Rolling Stone Encyclopedia of Rock & Roll,*

> The Velvets were unique in their intentional crudity, in their sense of beauty in ugliness and in their lyrics. In the age of flower power they spoke in no uncertain terms of social alienation, sexual deviancy, drug addiction, violence and hopelessness. Both in their sound and in their words, the songs evoked the exhilaration and destructiveness of modern urban life. (1983, 574)

Mark Fleischmann explains in *The New Trouser Press Record Guide:*

> Reed's influence on new wave began with the Velvet Underground's predilection for forbidden fruit—drugs, bizarre sex, suicide—in the lyrics, and raging chaos in the music. How could punk ever have occured without "Sister Ray" or "Heroin" as inspiring touchstones? (Robbins 1985, 327)

In 1966, the same year "Heroin" and "Venus in Furs" were recorded, "I'm a Believer," written by Neil Diamond and performed by the Monkees, was the number one hit song of the year. "I'm a Believer" expresses a sense of well-being and happiness about the future. The difference in the lyrical content of Reed's and Diamond's songs were greatly responsible for their varying degrees of commercial appeal.[4]

The musical structure of Reed's work departed from the 1960s pop compositional recipe in the length of his songs, their unpredictability, intentional incorporation of amateur quality, and aggressive style.

Commercially successful songs of the period generally ran from two to three minutes. The Velvet Underground placed no such strictures on the format of their music, and the length of their songs ranged from two minutes to seventeen minutes—almost one entire side of their *White Light/White Heat* (1967) album was one song.

Typical of Reed's compositions, "Heroin" also departs from the strict strophic form popular in 1960s rock-and-roll; the length of stanzas, both lyrically and in the musical phrasing, are uneven and unpredictable. Verses are set apart by improvised instrumental solos which, in recordings and live performances, employed a great deal of feedback and distortion performed at a deafening volume.

Technically, Reed accentuates the theme of heroin use by employing a rhythmical structure which imitates the heroin rush experienced by a user. The song begins at a moderate tempo, then accelerates in the second verse. The lull/rush/lull theme is repeated several times throughout the song. This is unusual in rock-and-roll compositions, which usually maintain a steady tempo from beginning to end, and adhere to a strophic form which gives a strong sense of predictability through sheer repetition.

Although the members of the Velvet Underground could not be called amateurs—having had extensive formal training—they deliberately employed an amateur quality in their music. By amateur quality I mean music which does not flaunt formal technical training. The Velvet Underground's music, both in live performances and recordings, reflects the band's interest in a spontaneous, unpolished sound. The recording of "European Son" on *The Velvet Underground and Nico* clearly exemplifies this. The majority of "European Son" consists of a fast, uninflected barrage of atonal sound, electronic feedback, and distortion dominated by Reed's electric guitar and Cale's custom-electrified viola. "Heroin" is another case in point. The exclusive repetition of two guitar chords—C and F—gives the song an amateur sound.

The method employed to record *The Velvet Underground and Nico* was designed to emphasize the spontaneity and excitement of a live performance. For the most part, the group did not take advantage of the elaborate recording techniques available to musicians in the studio. The entire album was completed in a mere eleven hours of studio time, with very little editing, mixing, or overdubbing (Malanga 1986, interview). Compare this with the Beatles' *Sergeant Pepper's Lonely Hearts Club Band* (1967), which took approximately 700 hours to record (Miller, ed. 1980, 183). *The Velvet Underground and Nico* was clearly not intended as a showcase for musical virtuosity or technical expertise. Rather, it documented the band's aesthetic sensibility: raw, unpolished, and aggressive.

John Rockwell, in *The Rolling Stone History of Rock & Roll,* describes the music of the Velvet Underground:

> The sound of The Velvet Underground came as a salutary shock to anyone used to the ever-slicker, artier concoctions of post-Sergeant Pepper rock. Twangy and raw, out of tune and deliberately monolithic of beat, marked by Reed's quavering vocalizing that sounded almost intuitively out of tune, violent yet tender in lyrics, full of cacophony and primitivism, this band was *different.* It proved that technical amateurishness and deliberate simplicity were no barrier to artistic communication; art rock could never again be equated with complexity, no matter what British progressive-rock bands enamored of the studio might think. (Miller 1980, 418)

Richard Goldstein, quoted on the inside cover of *The Velvet Underground and Nico,* described the music of the Velvet Underground as

a savage series of atonal thrusts and electronic feedback. The lyrics combine sadomasochistic frenzy with free association imagery. The whole sound seems to be the product of a secret marriage between Bob Dylan and the Marquis de Sade. (Verve Records, 1967)

The Velvet Underground's lyrical content, the length and unpredictability of their songs, and the intentional incorporation of amateur quality and aggressive musical style prevented the band from receiving the radio play neccessary to reach a large audience. This aggressive musical style, characterized by the use of electronic "noise" (feedback, dissonance, and uninflected rhythms), and in their live performances by tremendous volume[5] made them undesirable as performers in many popular rock venues. The relatively small cult following which developed around the Velvet Underground evolved from concerts at small New York clubs and cafés which offered an alternative to mainstream performance sensibilities. Later, the band's association with Andy Warhol, and infrequent one- or two-night performances at larger concert halls, expanded their audience.

The Velvet Underground had two bookings between the group's formation in November 1965 and the beginning of their association with Warhol in January 1966. First they opened for a band called the Myddle Class (later known as the King Bees) at Summit High School in Summit, New Jersey on 11 November 1965. Shortly before this performance, Angus MacLise left the band and was replaced by Maureen Tucker. The second Velvet Underground performance, arranged by pop music journalist Al Aronowitz, was a December residency at the Café Bizarre on West 3rd Street in Manhattan. Very little documentation exists for these early performances, though descriptions by band members and by people who attended the performances (Cutrone, in Bockris and Malanga 1983, 54; Malanga 1986, interview) reveal that at this time the Velvet Underground had already developed their unique performance style.

Just as the Velvet Underground's music intentionally lacked the high-tech polish and amiability popular with 1960s rock-and-roll audiences, so did their stage performances. Their fashion sensibility and stage demeanor departed from mainstream trends and anticipated punk style through blatant nonconformity and antisocial stance.

The Velvet Underground's fashion sensibility was the antithesis of commercial fashion trends of the late 1960s. The Velvet Underground did not groom themselves for mainstream consumption. They cultivated an intentionally rough look that served to distance them from the general public, using black leather jackets, black jeans, black vests, black boots, T-shirts, sweatshirts, and dark sunglasses to achieve an appearance that suggested the look of bohemian gang-

Figure 1. The Velvet Underground, circa 1965
Left to right: Sterling Morrison, Lou Reed, John Cale, and
Angus MacLise.
(Photo © by Gerard Malanga)

sters. The central idea was visual alienation. Nothing says "keep your distance" like dark sunglasses worn at night.

Stage demeanor was another important element that set the Velvet Underground apart from their contemporaries. Photographs and films of the Beatles, the Monkees, and other high-profile groups show smiling, energetic, and engaging youths. In figure 1 we see the Velvet Underground as a sullen group—unsmiling, undynamic, and aloof. The cool detachment, and minimal communication effected by sunglasses was reinforced by performance body language. The performers were even known to turn their backs on their audience. According to Ronnie Cutrone, who attended early Velvet Underground performances:

> Before the Velvet Underground almost without exception all groups came out and said, "Hey, we're gonna have a good time, let's get involved!," faced the audience, said, "This is a time of love, peace, happiness and sexual liberation and we're gonna have a great wonderful time." The Velvets on the other hand came out and turned their backs to the audience. (Bockris and Malanga 1983, 54)

The effect of the Velvet Underground on its audiences is vividly expressed in the following account by an audience member of a 1968 performance:

STANLEY THEATRE. PITTSBURGH, PA. 1968.

> The Velvet Underground are sinister and frightening. Their songs are about heroin, amphetamine, sex, and death: "I'm searching for my mainline, I couldn't hit it sideways." By the end of the first song, people are already beginning to leave. Lou sings "I'm waiting for my man/ 26 dollars in my hand/ Up to Lexington 125/ Feel sick and dirty/ More dead than alive/I'm waiting for my man." The sound is loud, driving, and hard. The words are tough, and Lou spits them out in an atonal, vicious manner. "Heroin" is next—Lou's classic anthem of drugs and decadence. The volume is ear splitting. A jet plane on stage would not have as profound an effect on the audience, which has by now been reduced by half. Heroin. Lou says he wants to nullify his life. There are people in the audience who can identify with this. There are people in the audience who are rapt—exhilarated at seeing and hearing the possibilities that they suspected were inherent in the rock genre but had never before been demonstrated. There are some, but not very many.
>
> "Sister Ray" is the last song. It goes on for a full half hour. Three chords: EEE, D, A, EEE, D, A, EEE, etc. The scene is eerie. Together the band creates an apocalyptic vision of eroticism, sadomasochism, and violence that is at once seductive and terrifying. The amplifiers feed back—the building seems to be shaking right to its foundations. The theatre is all but empty. (O'Hara 1984, unpublished manuscript)

While the Beatles were playing in sports stadiums and on the Ed Sullivan show, singing "I Want to Hold Your Hand" and "She Loves You," and the Monkees were appearing weekly on prime-time television, the Velvet Underground was playing seedy cellar bars (Café Bizzare) and avant-garde movie houses (Jonas Mekas' Filmmakers' Cinémathèque), singing songs about kinky sex and heroin. As their name so explicitly states, they were an underground band—far from the limelight of mass-media attention.

Ellen Willis, in a biography of Lou Reed distributed as public relations material by RCA Records, aptly summarizes the contibution of Lou Reed and the Velvet Underground to rock-and-roll history:

> Since the mid-sixties, virtually every significant development in rock-and-roll bore Lou Reed's imprint. As composer and lead singer for The Velvet Underground, Reed had more or less invented the genre of rock-and-roll—"avant-punk," as Robert Christgau aptly labeled it—that became the basis of the punk rock/new wave/new music explosion of the seventies.
>
> Because Reed's music so brilliantly evoked the bleakness . . . that seemed to define the seventies, and more recently the rebirth and revisionism that embody the eighties, it is easy to forget that his prophetic early work made a radical break with the prevailing musical and social atmosphere. The mid-sixties were above all an era of good feeling. The utopian mood spread from the west coast, even penetrating the skeptical marrow of New Yorkers. Who could resist getting high with a little help from the Beatles and the San Francisco acid rock bands, digging their promises of expanded consciousness, universal love, limitless possibility?
>
> In the midst of all this euphoria The Velvet Underground began performing in New York's East Village with Andy Warhol's mixed-media show, the *Exploding Plastic Inevitable*. Their publicity, which ran to phrases like "a total bombardment of the senses," suggested that the Velvets were yet another psychedelic band—in a way they were. But their brand of sensory bombardment could not have been more at odds with the era of good feeling. Their terrain was the city at its hardest and sleaziest. Their music was as painful as it was compelling, assaulting the ear with excruciating distortion and chaotic noise barely contained by the repetitive rhythms of rock-and-roll. Their themes were perversity, desperation and death. Instead of celebrating psychedelic trips they showed us the devastating power, horror and false transcendence of heroin addiction; they dared to intimate that sadomasochism might have more to do with their—and our—reality than universal love. (1986, 4)

From January 1966 to May 1967, Andy Warhol incorporated the Velvet Underground into a series of mixed-media shows which emphasized the band's aesthetic sensibilities. Through these performances, and his production of the Velvet Underground's first album, Warhol brought the band to the attention of a wider, more diversified audience while still expressing its nonconformist attitude.

In December 1965, Warhol heard the Velvet Underground at the Café Bizarre in Manhattan. Warhol, by that time already famous for his Pop paintings and experimental films, wanted to combine the Velvet Underground's music with his visual sensibility. According to Warhol:

> The Pop idea, after all, was that anybody could do anything, so naturally we were all trying to do it all. Nobody wanted to stay in one category, we all wanted to branch out into every creative thing we could. That's why when we met the Velvet Underground at the end of '65, we were all for getting into the music scene, too. (Warhol and Hackett 1980, 134)

In January 1966, the Velvet Underground began rehearsing at Warhol's studio, the Factory, then at 231 East 47th Street. The Factory was the gathering place for a continuous flow of painters, musicians, dancers, photographers, filmmakers, journalists, and hangers-on. At this time Warhol introduced Nico to the Velvet Underground. Nico, a German fashion model, actress, and aspiring singer, had recently arrived in New York from London where she had recorded a single, "The Last Mile," under the auspices of the Rolling Stones' manager Andrew Loog Oldham. In the early 1960s, she worked as a fashion model in London and Paris, and played a small role in Fellini's 1961 film *La Dolce Vita.* Warhol, interested in the visual and aural contrast between the Velvet Underground and Nico, convinced the Velvet Underground to use Nico as a lead singer. Warhol gave her equal billing in performances he booked for them and on the band's first album, *The Velvet Underground and Nico,* which he produced in 1967. Warhol declined to be interviewed about this period. In his book *POPism: The Warhol '60s,* a subjective documentation of the period coauthored with Pat Hackett, Nico is described as

> an incredible German beauty. She looked like she could have made the trip over right at the front of a Viking ship, she had that kind of face and body. When she first came on the scene she dressed very mod and spiffy in white wool pants, double-breasted blazers, beige cashmere turtlenecks. She had straight shoulder-length blond hair with bangs, blue eyes, full lips, wide cheekbones—the works. And she had this very strange way of speaking. People described her voice as everything from eery, to bland and smooth, to slow and hollow, to a "wind in a drainpipe," to an "IBM computer with a Garbo accent." She sounded the same strange way when she sang, too. (1980, 145)

Nico's blonde beauty and high fashion sensibility sharply contrasted with the rest of the band, who were rough and sinister-looking, dressed from head to toe in black (see fig. 2). Her low monotone voice was also a counterpoint to Reed's half-spoken lyrics and the band's high decibel distortion and feedback. Her recordings of "All Tomorrow's Parties" and "Femme Fatale" on *The Velvet Underground and Nico,* both written for her by Reed in 1966, exemplify her vocal style and provide a strong contrast to other Velvet Underground recordings of the period.

The addition of Nico as a highly visible "front (wo)man" for the Velvet Underground closely resembles McLaren's incorporation of Johnny Rotten (John Lydon) as lead singer for the Sex Pistols. Though the effects were quite different, the intentions of both managers were the same: to draw attention to the bands' nonconformist attitudes. Nico provided a strong contrast to the Velvet Underground, therefore exaggerating their aggressive, "streetwise" look and sound; Rotten served as a rebellious overstatement with his hyperactive stage presence and screaming vocals, thereby enhancing the Sex Pistols' shock value.

The Velvet Underground first performed with Nico on 13 January 1966 at the annual banquet of the New York Society for Clinical Psychiatry at Delmonico's restaurant in Manhattan, where Warhol was booked as a guest speaker. According to Warhol and Hackett:

Figure 2.   The Velvet Underground and Nico in Hollywood
Left to right: Andy Warhol, Nico, Danny Williams, Maureen
Tucker, Mary Woronov, Paul Morrisey, Lou Reed, Gerard
Malanga, and John Cale.
(Photo © by Gerard Malanga)

There were about three hundred psychiatrists and their mates and dates—and all they'd been told was that they were going to see movies after dinner. The second the main course was served, the Velvets started to blast and Nico started to wail. Gerard [Malanga] and Edie [Sedgewick] jumped up on the stage and started dancing, and the doors flew open and Jonas Mekas and Barbara Rubin with her crew of people with cameras and bright lights came storming into the room and rushing over to all the psychiatrists, asking them things like: "What does her vagina feel like?" "Is his penis big enough?"

They really were upset, and some of them started to leave, the ladies in their long dresses and the men in their black ties. As if the music—the feedback, actually—that the Velvets were playing wasn't enough to drive them out, the movie lights were blinding them and the questions were making them turn red and stutter because the kids wouldn't let up, they just kept on asking more. (1980, 146)

In a *New York Times* article appearing the next day, Grace Gluek wrote:

The act really came into its own about midway through the dinner . . . when "The Velvet Underground" swung into action. The high decibel sound, aptly described by Dr. Campbell as "a short-lived torture of cacophony," was a combination of rock 'n' roll and Egyptian belly-dance music.

The evening ended with a short talk by Jonas Mekas, film director and critic. But long before that, guests had begun to stream out. The reaction of the early departees was fairly unanimous. "Put it down as decadent Dada," said one. "It was ridiculous, outrageous, painful," said Dr. Harry Weinstock. "It seemed like a whole prison ward had escaped." (January 1966, 36)

The Delmonico's performance was the first of a series of mixed-media shows produced by Warhol which included the Velvet Underground. These shows, first billed as *Andy Warhol, Up-tight,* were later known as both *The Erupting Plastic Inevitable* and *The Exploding Plastic Inevitable.* The Warhol shows combined the Velvet Underground and Nico, Warhol's films, dancing, an elaborate light show, and often interviewing of the audience during performances. The various elements of these mixed-media shows bear a clear resemblance to the aesthetic sensibilities of the Velvet Underground.[6]

Warhol's films of this period, diametrically opposed to the cinematic sensibilities of Hollywood, paralleled the Velvet Underground's departure from mainstream tastes in popular music. The films contained both a technically unpolished style and subject matter offensive to the general public.

Warhol's films were low-budget by commercial standards. *Chelsea Girls* for instance, made during the summer of 1966, cost approximately $1,500, and involved little or no editing (Lester 1966, sec. D, 14). The result was more akin to home movies than to major-release films, which were already multimillion-dollar projects in 1966 and involved up to one year of editing (Louise Hamagami 1986, interview). Dennis Cipnic, in a 1972 *Sight and Sound* article, quoted Warhol in reference to the intentionally amateur quality of *Chelsea Girls:* "The camera work is bad, the lighting is awful, the technical work is terrible" (p. 159).

Chelsea Girls exemplifies Warhol's subject matter at its most objectionable to mainstream audiences. It deals graphically with drug addiction and homosexuality. Although articles in scholarly film journals place primary emphasis on Warhol's unorthodox projection and editing techniques (Ehrenstein 1966, 8; Battcock 1967, 363; Cipnic 1972, 159), they make reference to the preoccupation of the mass media with the subject matter of *Chelsea Girls.* Elenore Lester's 1966 *New York Times* review is an example of this mass-media concern:

> Andy Warhol's girls—Nico, Edie Sedgewick, and International Velvet—were all living in the Chelsea area last summer. And Andy . . . wanted to make this film. So he decided to call it "The Chelsea Girls." He had no particular theme for the film, nor did he have anything that might be seriously described as a script. The idea was just to show "people doing different things." So he got the girls together with some of his other friends who were around at the time and portrayed them cutting their hair, talking, injecting dope unhygenically into the seat of their tight blue jeans, playing lethargic multi-sex games. (1966, sec. D, 14)

Gluek summarizes the Warhol film aesthetic in another *New York Times* review:

> His films, peopled by dope addicts, deviates, hustlers and assorted weirdos engaged in interminable non-action, exactly reverse the glossy clichés of Hollywood movies, structured on tight plot lines and acted by Beautiful People. (June 1966, sec. E, 6)

At least two films were made of Warhol's mixed-media shows: *Andy Warhol's Exploding Plastic Inevitable* (1966) and *Live at the Balloon Farm* (1966).

Dance was a consistent element in Warhol's mixed-media shows and clearly underlined the Velvet Underground's and Warhol's allusions to sexual deviancy. Gerard Malanga was the center of attention here. Malanga, an underground film actor who appeared in Warhol's *Vinyl* and *Chelsea Girls* became a staple of the show with what became known as his "whip dance," performed onstage in front of the band. According to Malanga and Bockris, Malanga

> danced in black leather pants with his whip, eerily mirroring The Velvet's style with his sinuous, mesmeric movements, which resembled a cross between the Frug and an Egyptian belly dance. (1983, 10)

Besides Malanga, assorted members of the Warhol entourage (including, among others, Edie Sedgewick, Mary Woronov, and Ronnie Cutrone) performed improvised dances at various times both on- and offstage. Never as compelling as Malanga with his thirteen-foot whip, these dancers were nonetheless important members of the troupe. According to Malanga in a 1986 interview, none of the dancers who performed with the *Exploding Plastic Inevitable* had any formal dance training.

The visual intensity of Warhol's light show equalled the aural intensity of the Velvet Underground's music. Lighting consisted of improvised workings of brightly colored spotlights, strobe lights, floodlights, slide projectors, flashlights, phosphorescent tape, and any other available light source as budget and the performing space allowed, as well as Warhol's films. Images were superimposed upon one another and shown randomly over performers, audience members, walls, ceiling, and floor. John Wilcock described the effect in an *East Village Other* article:

> Onstage . . . the movie *Couch* was being projected. A pair of other projectors up in the balcony went into action beaming two different movies onto the narrow strips of wall beside the stage. A colored spotlight onstage focused onto the mirrored ball that revolved in the ceiling sending pinpoints of light . . . around the room. A plastic globe glowed in cycles of changing pastel colors. Colored floodlights stabbed out from the corners, caressing the dancers with beams of green, orange, purple. *Vinyl* was playing on the screen . . . but it was being obscured by brightly colored slides and patterns from two slide machines operated by Jacki Casson. Slashes of red and blue, squares of black and white, rows of dancing dots covered the walls, the ceiling, the dancers. From up front, by the stage, the hall was a frantic, frenzied fandango of action: the lights flashing on and off, the fragmented pieces of movies, the colored patterns and slides sweeping the mirrored walls, the steady white beams of balcony projectors, the Sylvania strip lighting writhing on the floor, flashing on and off like a demented snake who's swallowed phosphorous, the foot-long flashlights of Gerard Malanga randomly stabbing the darkened hall. (1966, 5)

Audience interviews during performances were intentional provocations. Just as the Velvet Underground provoked uneasiness in many observers through their lyrical content, abrasive sound, and aggressive looks, Barbara Rubin and other interviewers evoked uneasiness in *Andy Warhol, Up-tight* audiences by using obscene language, asking embarrassing questions, and filming the audience's responses. Bockris and Malanga describe an interview during a February 1966 performance:

> Barbara Rubin rushed down the aisle with her sun-gun glaring into their faces screaming questions like "Is your penis big enough?" and "Does he eat you out?" It was Barbara who had suggested the *Andy Warhol, Up-tight* name and developed the concept of making people uptight rather than relaxed by filming their responses with her movie camera. (1983, 7)

In February 1966, Warhol booked a week of performances (8–13 February) for *Andy Warhol, Up-tight* at Jonas Mekas' Filmmaker's Cinémathèque, a small basement movie house at 125 West 41st Street which showcased noncommercial filmmakers. Bockris and Malanga describe the performance in some detail and give a clear idea of what Warhol's mixed-media shows were like:

> After two 35-minute reels of [Warhol's film] *Lupe*, The Velvet Underground and Nico walked onto the stage in front of the movie screen and began to tune up in the dark. Andy, who was working one movie projector, now trained a silent version of *Vinyl*, his interpretation of *A*

Clockwork Orange, starring Gerard Malanga as a juvenile delinquent, on the screen. Superimposed on this by another movie projector run by Paul Morrissey were close-up shots of Nico singing "I'll Keep It with Mine" by Bob Dylan. Looking ghostly in the flickering movie lights, Nico on stage picked up the song from Nico on screen and the band joined in behind her. Then, as The Velvet Underground went into "Venus in Furs," Gerard Malanga and Edie Sedgewick moved to centre stage and began gyrating in a free form dance pattern. The whole ensemble was now playing in front of two movies *Vinyl* and *The Velvet Underground and Nico: A Symphony of Sound* being shown silently next to each other. While Nat Finklestein circulated taking uptight photographs . . . , Danny Williams, the Factory's Harvard grad electrician, began to project color slides over the band and the films. Suddenly and unexpectedly, a huge spotlight came crashing down and shone directly on the audience. As The Velvets went into "Run Run Run," Lou leaned into his guitar grinning maniacally in black dungarees, a rumpled jacket over a black T-shirt and high-heel boots. John Cale was hunkered over his viola in a black suit with a rhinestone choke necklace designed by Kenny Jay Lane in the shape of a snake, while Nico, tall, thin, hauntingly beautiful, stood silhouetted alone in a chic white pants suit. Maureen Tucker, the innocent looking drummer whose sex nobody could at first discern, stood behind her bass drum using tom tom mallets to hit it with machine-like precision, while rhythm and lead guitarist extraordinaire Sterling Morrison, all in black, stood rock still in the midst of this terrible discordant-chaotic-flashing commotion of light, sound, and sight. For the most part the audience sat there too stunned to think or react. The music was supersonic and very loud. The Velvets turned their amps up as high as they could go. The effect vibrated all through the audience. (1983, 7)

In April 1966, Warhol leased the Open Stage in Manhattan for a month of performances. The Open Stage was a large dance hall located on the third floor of the old Polish National Social Hall, known as the Dom (Polish for "home"), at 23 St. Mark's Place. The name of the show was changed at this point from *Andy Warhol, Up-tight* to *The Erupting Plastic Inevitable* and then to *The Exploding Plastic Inevitable.* A half-page ad in *The Village Voice* (7 April 1966, 29) ran:

Come Blow Your Mind
the Silver Dream Factory presents the first
EXPLODING PLASTIC INEVITABLE
with
Andy Warhol
The Velvet Underground
and
Nico

Superstars Gerard Malanga and Mary Woronov on Films
on Stage on Vinyl

Live Music, Dancing, Ultra Sounds, Visions, Lightworks by Danny Williams, Color Slides by Jackie Cassen, Discotheque, Refreshments, Ingrid Superstar, Food, Celebrities, and Movies including: *Vinyl, Sleep, Eat, Kiss, Empire, Whips, Faces, Harlot, Hedy, Couch, Banana,* etc., etc., etc. All in the same place at the same time.

At the Open Stage 23 St. Mark's Place (Bet. 2nd and
3rd) 9–2 Nitely

According to Warhol and Hackett, the day after the sublet papers were signed on the dance hall,

> we were down there painting the place white so we could project movies and slides on the walls. We started dragging prop-type odds and ends over from the Factory—five movie projectors, five carousel-type projectors where the image changes every ten seconds and where, if you put two images together, they bounce. These colored things would go on top of the five movies, and sometimes we'd let the sound tracks come through. We also brought down one of those big revolving speakeasy mirrored balls—we had it lying around the Factory and we thought it would be great to bring those back. We had a guy come down with more spotlights and strobes that we wanted to rent—we were going to shine them on the Velvets and all around the audience during the show. Of course, we had no idea if people would come all the way down to St. Mark's Place for night life. All the downtown action had always been in the West Village—the East Village was Babushkaville. But by renting the Dom ourselves, we didn't have to worry about whether "management" liked us or not, we could just do whatever we wanted to. And the Velvets were thrilled—in the Dom, the "house band" finally found a house. (1980, 156)

When Warhol's lease on the Dom expired 30 April 1966, *The Exploding Plastic Inevitable* gave a series of performances outside New York City. No precise records of performance bookings exist from this period, though according to Bockris and Malanga (1983) and Warhol and Hackett (1980) the show played in the following cities chronologically between May and September 1966: Los Angeles; San Francisco; Chicago; and Provincetown, Mass.

From 24 September to 23 October 1966, *The Exploding Plastic Inevitable* returned to the Dom for a month of Friday and Saturday night performances. Al Grossman and Oliver Coquelin had taken a new lease on the Dom while the *Exploding Plastic Inevitable* was on tour and reopened it in the fall of 1966 as a new club called The Balloon Farm (later known as the Electric Circus when the management changed again in April 1967). One of the very few reviews written on the *Exploding Plastic Inevitable* appeared in the "Scenes" column of the *Village Voice* at this time:

> As usual there is a dizzying amount of visual stuff: psychedelic patterns, strobes, spotlights, bubble machine, and the long, slow blow-ups of . . . people . . . in inscrutable staring contest with the camera. Plus the screeching of the electronic [viola], rock-and-roll, and ear splitting drums. (22 September 1966, 28)

Records of *Exploding Plastic Inevitable* performances after the last Balloon Farm show are extremely sketchy. Bockris and Malanga (1983) and Warhol and Hackett (1980) indicate that the show toured extensively throughout the United States and Canada from October to December 1966. The following is a list of cities (by no means exhaustive) *The Exploding Plastic Inevitable* played during this period: Boston; Detroit; Cleveland; Cincinnati; Columbus, Ohio; Pittsburgh; and Hamilton, Ontario, Canada.

In March 1967, the Velvet Underground's first album, *The Velvet Underground and Nico,* was released by Verve Records, a division of Metro-Goldwyn-Mayer (MGM). Recorded during the summer of 1966, its release had been delayed due to the company's objection to the language and subject matter of such songs as "Heroin" (the lyrics "you can all go take a fucking walk" were changed to "you can all go take a walk"), "Venus in Furs," and "Waiting for the Man." Release of the album was also delayed because of the difficulty and expense of producing the Warhol-designed album cover which included a picture of a banana with a stick-on, peelable skin. Furthermore, Eric Emerson, whose photograph originally appeared on the back cover in a still from *Chelsea Girls,* demanded royalties, which MGM refused to pay, and the cover had to be reprinted sans Emerson.

The Velvet Underground and Nico received virtually no radio play because of its objectionable content and harsh sound. According to Ronnie Cutrone:

> With songs like "Heroin" you're certainly not going to get any radio play in 1967. The Beatles were singing about broken relationships and "all you need is love." "Sympathy for the Devil" was the heaviest the Rolling Stones ever got. And then you get a group coming out and saying, "When I'm rushing on my run/I feel just like Jesus' son" you're not going to get any radio play—it's as simple as that. (Bockris and Malanga 1983, 76)

Despite lack of airplay, the album (barely) made the *Billboard* charts, reaching number 171 (out of a possible 200)[7] in 1967. Sales figures for *The Velvet Underground and Nico* are unavailable[8] but were considered low by the recording industry (Blackwood 1986, interview). Nonetheless, *The Velvet Underground and Nico* did extend the Velvet Underground's audience beyond a strictly live performance following and was essential in establishing the band's faithful, albeit small, cult following.

Although the notoriety attained by the Velvet Underground through the album and live performances was noteworthy for performers in the avant-garde performing arts community, it was limited by commercial standards. For instance the Beatles' album, *Sergeant Pepper's Lonely Hearts Club Band,* released the same year as *The Velvet Underground and Nico,* was number one on the *Billboard* charts in 1967, and sold over one million copies. The Beatles' highly publicized international tours at sports stadiums and large concert halls put them in an entirely different league than the Velvet Underground, whose performances were limited to small night clubs and occasional one- or two-night stands at larger concert halls.

From 24 March to 1 May 1967, the *Exploding Plastic Inevitable* gave a month of weekend performances at the Gymnasium at 42 East 71st Street in Manhattan. The club was actually an old gymnasium, with a minimal conversion to allow for a small stage for the band and the light show. According to Warhol, "We left it exactly as it was, with the mats, parallel bars, weights, straps, and barbells" (Warhol and Hackett 1980, 209).

The Exploding Plastic Inevitable gave its last performance in May 1967 at the Scene at 301 West 46th Street in Manhattan.[9] By this time, multimedia shows had become popular with large audiences and were a major component in the psychedelia craze sweeping the country's youth counterculture. From September to December 1966, Timothy Leary had given his landmark "Celebration" performances in New York, meant to parallel an LSD trip; the San Francisco Acid Tests were a staple of the Haight-Ashbury scene; and countless clubs specializing in multimedia shows opened up all over the country. In New York, the *Village Voice* and *East Village Other* newspapers were rife with advertisements for clubs such as the Electro Media Theatre, the Hip Trip, and the Electric Circus. Multimedia shows had become so commercially viable that companies like Celestron Associates in New York specialized in creating lighting systems for "total environment clubs"(*Village Voice,* 11 May 1967, 38).

With the emphasis on audience involvement at these clubs, the performer/audience distinction began to blur. The *Exploding Plastic Inevitable* felt that their role as performers was no longer necessary in such an environment, and that the commercialization of multimedia shows had made the genre uninteresting. Ronnie Cutrone explains:

> The last time we played as The E.P.I. . . . was in May 1967 at the Steve Paul's Scene. Before this people came to watch The E.P.I. dance and play, they were entertained, and got a show. But when we played at the Scene I remember Gerard, Mary and I were dancing and the audience came on stage with us and totally took over. Everybody became part of The E.P.I. It was a bit sad, because we couldn't keep our glory on stage. All of a sudden there were no dancers, there was no show; the music had just taken everybody at that point . . . by then light shows had become such a cliché that it was over for us . . . the impact was over, the shock was over. (Bockris and Malanga 1983, 78)

Through the New York performances and national tours of Warhol's mixed-media shows, and the release of *The Velvet Underground and Nico,* the Velvet Underground was brought to the attention of a wider audience. Without the public exposure secured by Warhol, the Velvet Underground may well have remained an isolated oddity rather than becoming a progenitor of a new subcultural style.

The direct influence of Lou Reed and the Velvet Underground on the punk-rock movement in England is exemplified by their prominent positions in record charts compiled by punk fans in small publications called fanzines.[10] Record charts in fanzines were compiled on the criteria of record sales to, and nominations by, readers. Though these charts by no means reflect the tastes of mainstream rock-and-roll audiences, they are invaluable in establishing Reed's and the Velvet Underground's popularity within the punk-rock audience. For instance, the second issue of *Ripped and Torn* (January 1977), one of the most widely circulated punk fanzines, contains two top twenty record charts—one for singles and one for albums. The singles chart gives "Foggy Notion" by the Velvet Underground the number five position. The album chart lists six entries (including the number one position) for Lou Reed and/or the Velvet Underground, and includes every Velvet Underground album recorded at the time of the fanzine's publication. The prominence of Lou Reed and the Velvet Underground in charts such as this is especially noteworthy since the recordings were up to ten years old at the time of the chart's publication. British fanzines also frequently featured articles and record reviews concerning Lou Reed and/or the Velvet Underground (e.g., *Sniffin' Glue,* September 1976, no. 3, p. 9; *Sniffin' Glue,* October 1976, no. 4, p. 6; *Heat,* October/November 1977, p. 6). This is evidence not only of these musicians' influence on punk-rock aesthetics, but also of the enduring appeal of their work.

2

Glitter Rock and the New York Dolls: Gender Bending and Apocalyptic Vision

Glitter rock (also known as glam rock) developed simultaneously in the United States and Great Britain in the early 1970s. It gained recognition among rock-and-roll audiences for confusing traditional images of gender distinction and incorporating subject matter deemed offensive to the general public. As an affront to mainstream sensibilities, these elements of glitter rock were appropriated and elaborated upon by later punk rockers and provided much of the material from which punk drew its specific symbols of rebellion.

Little has been written about glitter rock as a specific movement (see Pareles and Romanowski 1983, 218; and Hebdige 1979, 59), and the term is used loosely to refer to a number of performers (e.g., Marc Bolan, David Bowie, Roxy Music, Wayne County, Kiss, the New York Dolls) whose lyrical content, musical structure, stage performance, and commercial appeal vary widely. However, the common denominators of glitter rock—sexual ambiguity and controversial subject matter—are the genre's most important elements in terms of its contribution to the development of punk rock.

Glitter rock confounded traditional images of gender distinction through one or more of the following techniques: androgyny, transvestism, and parody of sexual stereotypes (e.g., tongue-in-cheek impersonations of Marilyn Monroe and Mick Jagger). Glitter rock was dominated by male performers with a propensity toward the use of cosmetics, female clothing, and unisex attire. The stage personas of various performers (see fig. 3) departed from traditional dress codes of rock-and-roll machismo as set forth by such performers as Elvis Presley and the Rolling Stones as well as pedestrian gender-distinct fashions.

Glitter rock's treatment of controversial subject matter amplified the precedent set by the Velvet Underground and Andy Warhol. While the Velvet Underground and Warhol addressed issues on a personal level (i.e., drug abuse and sexual deviancy), glitter rock addressed issues in a larger sociopolitical arena. Glitter rock expanded the vocabulary of alienation to include issues encompass-

Figure 3. Wayne County Performing in Drag, circa 1974
(Photo © by Mark Ivins)

ing a broader social context. Nazism and nuclear holocaust, for example, were used as thematic material for songs.

This escalating interest in shock value among rock-and-roll performers is important in tracing the evolution of punk. As images became familiar to audiences, their impact weakened and newer, more extreme methods were employed. Lyrical allusions to transvestism, for instance, gave way to musicians actually performing in drag. Likewise, subject matter became more extreme: When sadomasochism became passé, glitter rockers began singing about the end of the biosphere.

Ironically, while glitter rock took gender ambiguity and disturbing subject matter to extremes, its message was expressed in a commercially viable musical structure, incorporating strophic form, melodic arrangements, and sophisticated recording techniques. This achieved the polished, technically sophisticated sound admired by popular music audiences and served as a compromise for performers with rebellious social attitudes who also wanted commercial success. Unlike the Velvet Underground, who delivered disturbing subject matter within an unfamiliar, unlistenable (to mainstream audiences) musical structure, glitter rockers delivered disturbing subject matter within a familiar, listenable one. By adhering to acceptable standards of popular musical form, glitter rock themes became less threatening to their audiences. As we shall see, the lyrical medicine was given with a lump of structural sugar.

Glitter rock was a short-lived (roughly 1972–75) but influential phenomenon. The origins of glitter rock can be traced directly to Lou Reed's association with Andy Warhol and his Factory entourage, and to British performer-musician David Bowie. Throughout the late 1960s, Warhol and the Velvet Underground shared a mutual interest in sexual deviancy as thematic material, as evidenced by Warhol's films and Reed's songs. During this time, Warhol was also associated with a number of transvestites—most notably Candy Darling, Jackie Curtis, and Holly Woodlawn—who gained notoriety in New York avant-garde circles through their appearances in Warhol's film *Flesh* (1969, filmed by Paul Morrissey), their frequent presence at the Factory, and later (1973–75) performances at New York nightclubs such as Club 82 and Cabaret in the Sky. Warhol was greatly responsible (along with the sexual revolution of the 1960s and an emerging gay liberation movement) for bringing transvestism and gender confusion out of their marginal context into the limelight of media attention. In *POPism: The Warhol '60s* Warhol explains:

As late as '67 drag queens still weren't accepted in the mainstream freak circles. They were still hanging around where they'd always hung around—on the fringes, around the big cities, usually in crummy little hotels, sticking to their own circles—outcasts with bad teeth and body odor and cheap makeup and creepy clothes. But then, just as drugs had come into the average person's life, sexual blurs did too, and people began identifying a little more with drag queens, seeing them more as "sexual radicals" than as depressing losers. That's how in '68, after so many years of being repelled by them, people started accepting drag queens—even courting them, inviting them everywhere. (Warhol and Hackett 1980, 223)

Although transvestism was interesting and to some degree acceptable (usually from a non-particapatory distance) in experimental art circles, it was and still is unacceptable to the cultural mainstream. Therefore it became prime material for underground-rock musicians preoccupied with subject matter and behavior which shocked the middle class.[1]

In the United States, the interest in gender confusion made its leap from avant-garde art to the rock-and-roll world in part via Lou Reed. After leaving the Velvet Underground in 1970, Reed began incorporating transvestism into his lyrical content. This was an extension of his earlier interest in sadomasochism as an allusion to sexual deviancy, a development probably inspired by Warhol. In 1971 Reed wrote "Walk on the Wild Side" for a stage production of Nelson Algren's novel of the same name (1956). The song is about the lives of several transvestites Reed met at the Factory in 1968.

Despite the song's allusions to transvestism, oral sex, and drugs, "Walk on the Wild Side" became Reed's first hit song, rating number 31 on the *Billboard* Hot 100 in 1973 and receiving frequent national radio play.[2] The song's success was due to its upbeat rhythm and catchy melody (as opposed to the Velvet Underground's frequent use of distortion, feedback, and unmelodic sound) rather than its lyrical content. By placing the lyrics of "Walk on the Wild Side" within a popular musical structure, Reed laid the groundwork for tolerance of gender blurring and other previously unnacceptable subject matter by mainstream audiences.

While Reed and Warhol's Factory group precipitated an interest in gender roles and transvestism in American popular music, it was David Bowie, a British rock musician, who honed this interest into a commercially successful rock genre. Bowie was influenced in the late 1960s by the Velvet Underground (an influence made apparent by Bowie's incorporation of Reed's song "Waiting for the Man" into his 1967 British concert series), and Marc Bolan (also known as T. Rex), a British musician who performed with a band called Tyrannosaurus Rex from 1967 to 1975. Although Bolan's lyrics did not deal with gender distinctions, he became known in popular music circles for his feminine stage presence: long hair, cosmetics, and sequined jackets. Bowie, who occasionally performed with Bolan during the late 1960s, took Bolan's concept further, appearing at concerts and on the cover of his 1970 album *The Man Who Sold the World* wearing a dress.

In early 1971, while on a United States tour, Bowie met Reed and Warhol and visited the Factory. Two of the songs on Bowie's *Hunky Dory* album, released in November 1971, were inspired by the Velvet Underground and

Warhol's Factory scene: "Queen Bitch" is a tribute to the Velvet Underground (Pareles and Romanowski 1983, 61; Miller 1976, 387; Carr and Murray 1981, 41; Willis, 6)—an emulation of Reed's half-spoken vocal style, simple melodies, and allusions to transvestism; "Andy Warhol" makes reference to Warhol's films and life at the Factory.

In May 1972, Bowie appeared on stage in the character of the flamboyant Ziggy Stardust. This first in a series of performance alter egos created by Bowie launched him to international fame. The influence of Bolan, Reed, and Warhol was apparent. Ziggy was an elegant, exotic, androgynous creature with delicate features and petite stature; short, spiky orange hair; painted face; painted fingernails; and clinging, bespangled, futuristic costumes. Bowie brought an element of sexual ambiguity to rock that it had never seen before. His publicly proclaimed bisexuality (*Melody Maker*, 22 January 1972, 1) further added to his exotic persona. According to Hebdige:

> Bowie, . . . in a series of "camp" incarnations (Ziggy Stardust, Aladdin Sane, Mr. Newton, the Thin White Duke, and more depressingly the Blond Führer) achieved something of a cult status in the early '70s. He attracted a mass youth . . . audience and set up a number of visual precedents in terms of personal appearance (makeup, dyed hair, etc.) which created a new sexually ambiguous image for those youngsters willing and brave enough to challenge the notoriously pedestrian stereotypes conventionally available to working-class men and women. (1979, 60)

Bowie's androgynous look, his short spiky hair with its deliberately unconvincing dye job, and his elaborate use of cosmetics are three elements of his physical appearance which were later preempted and elaborated upon by punk rockers.

An important element of Bowie's style was the fact that he maintained the Ziggy Stardust look both on- and offstage, appearing in public in full costume and makeup. At the height of the Ziggy Stardust craze (1972), Bowie's fans began to emulate him, appearing at concerts and on city streets as Ziggy lookalikes. While rock-and-roll performers and fans have always used fashion as a medium to express nonconformist attitudes, the glitter rock phenomenon was an extreme. According to Polhemus and Procter:

> Groups such as Kiss don't really shake up the status quo because it's all clearly just for the stage. This sort of tongue-in-cheek makeup is safe because it's just theatre, but David Bowie in the early seventies was something else. The man was serious. Parents who hadn't raised their sons to wear lipstick, pan-cake [makeup] and eye shadow, or their daughters to fancy such abominations were scared. (1984, 75)

By taking bizarre personal appearance usually reserved for stage performance to the streets, Bowie's impact was double-edged. What was considered strange enough in the context of theatrical performance was even stranger in a pedestrian context. This set a precedent for punk rock, which was focused as much on the streets of London as on the stages of small nightclubs.

In June 1972, Bowie recorded *The Rise and Fall of Ziggy Stardust and the Spiders from Mars.* The album chronicled the arrival of a space-age messiah (Ziggy Stardust), offering hope to a dying world through rock-and-roll. Anthony Rivers, in *Starzone* (1981) magazine, explains the story:

> The [songs] work as a sequence. "Ziggy" opened with "Five Years"—the world has but that time to live, and we hear different people's reactions to this, all seen through Ziggy's eyes. Ziggy was a parody of the conventional, the definitve rock 'n' roll star. We witness his progress from playing for peanuts in sleazy bar-rooms ("Lady Stardust") . . . to being on the brink of success ("Star" and "Hang onto Yourself") eventually to rise to the ultimate heights of superstardom. And, as so very often happens in real life, [he] finds he can't cope with the fame and finally commits suicide ("Rock and Roll Suicide").

Bowie's interest in doomsday imagery, so clearly expressed in *The Rise and Fall of Ziggy Stardust and the Spiders from Mars,* had already been established on his 1970 album, *The Man Who Sold the World,* when he sang "The World is doomed. We can't make it any better." The message implicit in Bowie's songs from this period anticipated the punk anthem "No Future" by at least four years.

As Reed had done with "Walk on the Wild Side," Bowie related his message through a readily acceptable strophic, melodic structure. Bowie's lyrical content, however, was not limited to the marginal realm of sexual deviancy and drug abuse that Reed's was. Rather, it dealt with the universal problem presented by the awareness of possible annihilation of the human species through nuclear catastrophe.

Bowie's thematic interest in global catastrophe and apocalyptic vision was later reinforced by his subsequent incarnations as Aladdin Sane and the Thin White Duke. Aladdin Sane was an extension of the Ziggy Stardust persona —a futuristic androgyne who, on the album *Aladdin Sane* (1973), encounters a world on the brink of annihilation. The Thin White Duke was an alter ego adopted for Bowie's *Station to Station* album (1976). The "mad aristocrat," as Carr and Murray (1981, 79) called him, outraged music audiences for his apparent approval of Nazism in trade magazine interviews (Charlesworth 1983, 1629).

As a huge commercial success,[3] Bowie brought gender blurring and doomsday imagery to a vast, accepting audience, in effect commercializing the heretofore uncommercial. While Bowie provided a rich source of raw material upon which the punk-rock movement would later draw, he also proved ultimately to be an an authority figure against which it rebelled: punk rockers embraced Bowie's interests in gender ambiguity and doomsday imagery, while rejecting what they perceived as a distasteful interest in commercial appeal and monetary gain.

In the summer of 1972, Reed hired Bowie to produce his album *Transformer* (released in November 1972), which contained the song "Walk on the Wild Side." Reed also gave a series of performances in London. According to Willis:

> Reed's performances in London in the summer of 1972, made apparent the influence of Bowie's theatrical, sexually ambiguous aesthetic: Lou wore black eye makeup, black lipstick and a black velvet suit with rhinestone trimmings. The album, *Transformer,* referred directly and explicitly to gay life and transvestism. (1980, 6)

Becoming as much a persona chameleon as Bowie, Reed's appearance underwent another drastic transformation in 1973. After the September release of his next album, *Berlin,* Reed shed his androgynous look for one clearly related to *Berlin*'s thematic allusions to the atrocities of wartime Germany. Diana Clapton describes Reed's dramatic metamorphosis in her book *Lou Reed and the Velvet Underground:*

> Physically, a relatively robust Reed led into [performances] . . . in stunning black leather, whiteface, Biba black nail polish and matching lipstick, black eye liner and long, curly locks. He looked like a sexy, rabid wolverine. Within a few weeks his hair had been shorn in a crew-cut iron cross and he resembled an upwardly-mobile member of the Hitler jugend. Poor diet had made his figure lean; around this he wrapped bicycle chains and heavy buckles from boutiques such as Greenwich Village's Pleasure Chest. (1982, 60)

Reed's solo career, like Bowie's, foreshadowed punk in two ways. First, Reed blurred the distinctions between stage persona and private citizen by appearing in public in the same guise in which he appeared on stage. Second, by making the thematic leap from sexual deviancy to Nazism, Reed began to address "no future" as an issue with which a larger audience could identify.

This is not to say that all the imagery employed by such performers was meant to be taken at face value. It is clear in Bowie's songs that his doomsday imagery did not imply approval of nuclear war. Likewise, Reed's references to Nazi Germany, when considered in the total context of his albums and stage performance, are not an endorsement of fascism. Rather, these allusions were meant to bring attention to social problems—to offer a candid look at the oppression that society permits, whether it be on the grounds of sexual preference, race, religion, or aesthetic values.

The New York Dolls, a New York–based glitter rock band, were another important influence in the development of punk rock. Like Reed and Bowie, their sexually ambiguous appearance, bizarre fashions, technical amateurishness, and antagonistic attitude clearly anticipated the punk aesthetic. The New York Dolls were managed in 1975 by Malcolm McLaren, who shortly thereafter masterminded the Sex Pistols—first and most notorious of the punk bands. This link between the New York-based New York Dolls and the London-based Sex Pistols was essential in establishing the direct influence of New York underground rock bands on the impending British punk subculture.

The New York Dolls were formed in February 1972 in New York City. The original line-up included Johnny Thunders (guitar, vocals), Billy Murcia (drums), David Johansen (vocals), Arthur Kane (bass), and Rick Rivets (guitar). Rivets left the band in March 1972 and was replaced by Sylvain Sylvain.[4]

During the winter and spring of 1972, the New York Dolls played a number of small rock venues in New York, including Kenny's Castaways, the Diplomat Hotel, and Max's Kansas City. However, it was not until the band secured a four-month residency of Tuesday night performances at the Mercer Arts Center, from April to July 1972, that they began to attract an enthusiastic local following.

The Mercer Arts Center, in operation during 1972 and 1973, was an assemblage of boutiques and performance spaces located in the Broadway Central Hotel at Broadway and West Fourth Street in Manhattan. Among the most notable of the Mercer Arts Center venues were the Kitchen (located in the hotel's original kitchen), a leading forum for experimental music and video art now located at 512 West 19th Street, and the Oscar Wilde Room, a performance space devoted to New York glitter-rock bands such as Wayne County, Eric Emerson, Teenage Lust, Ruby and the Rednecks, Queen Elizabeth, Kiss, and the New York Dolls.

The New York Dolls affected a sexually ambiguous appearance onstage through their androgynous use of cosmetics, long hair, and fancy dress. Bob and Nadya Gruen's videotapes of New York Dolls performances (*The New York Dolls: Lookin' for a Kiss* 1973; and *Don Kirshner's Rock Concert: The New York Dolls* 1974) show the band wearing pancake makeup, rouge, eyeshadow, mascara, and lipstick. Their long, curly hair is teased out into copious masses or, in the case of Johansen, tied into ponytails or elaborate coiffures. The band is also dressed in an eclectic assortment of clothing which transcends standard definitions of gender: platform-heeled boots, leather jackets and pants, leopard-skin jumpsuits, sequined leotards, fishnet stockings, fringed cowboy shirts and pants, scarves, halter tops, suit jackets and vests, bow ties, bracelets, and a variety of hats (bowlers, cowboy hats, etc.).

The band maintained this fashion sensibility both on- and offstage, surprising onlookers not only within a performance context, but within a pedestrian one as well. According to Peter Jordan, the group's sound engineer throughout their career and bass player for the band from 1972 to 1977: "The 'normal' Dolls used to dress the same way they dressed on stage . . . it was virtually the same.

Figure 4.   The New York Dolls, circa 1974
(Photo © by Bob Gruen)

To this day it would be unusual to see anyone dressed that way on the street"
(1986, interview).

While the New York Dolls followed the precedent set by David Bowie and
Lou Reed in blurring gender distinctions and in taking theatrical fashions to the
street, their fashion sensibility was unique. Though Bowie's and Reed's androgynous looks departed from the 1970s fashion status quo, they drew on
elements of previously established fashion trends: Bowie wore futuristic clothing carefully designed to look like the epitome of "space age" high fashion;
Reed's black leather outlaw attire was by the 1970s already an established mode
of dress for many rock-and-roll musicians. The New York Dolls, on the other
hand, incorporated stylistic elements which had never before been used by rock
bands. The deliberate garishness of the band's appearance, and their interest in
expanding the parameters of outrageousness in both rock-and-roll stage attire
and pedestrian fashions foreshadowed the punk movement by at least two years.

The New York Dolls stressed gender ambiguity in their act through
Johansen's parodies of Mick Jagger and Elvis Presley. Jagger and Presley are
generally considered by popular music fans to epitomize rock-and-roll machismo. By presenting these stars as foppish androgynes, Johansen brought
attention to his own sexually ambiguous appearance, "effectively removing
visual barriers between straight and gay suggestiveness" (Kirby 1972, 61). Ed
McCormack described a 1972 Mercer Arts Center performance in a *Rolling
Stone* review:

> Tonight David has his shoulder-length pageboy tied up tightly, his puff ball bangs pinned up
> into a bun that is a parody of a huge Elvis pompadour. The tackiest Miami Beach dowager's
> jumpsuit is pulled over his skinny, nubile body like a gold lamé prophylactic. It is open all the
> way down to his navel . . . as he flings himself around the stage on his six-inch platform-heeled
> open-toed Minnie Mouse mules . . . [and] spits the words into the phallic mike. (1972, 14)

While the New York Dolls confounded traditional images of gender distinction in their stage performance, they, unlike Bowie and Reed, did not make
public allusions to homosexual private lives. More akin to Bowie's and Reed's
references to doomsday imagery, illicit drug use, and sadomasochism, gender
ambiguity was not meant to be taken at face value. Gender blurring and outrageous attire were simply means by which to shock the general public and show
rock audiences something they had never seen before.

The New York Dolls also rebelled against mainstream trends by presenting
music which was deliberately amateurish in quality. While most glitter rock
bands leaned toward a technically polished sound, the New York Dolls did not.
With little training[5] and uncomplicated musical structures, the band was noted
more for its enthusiastic presence and bizarre fashions than its technical expertise (D.C.E. 1974, 3; Naha 1973, 10; Nelson 1985, 130). Like the Velvet

Figure 5.   The New York Dolls, circa 1974
(Photo © by Bob Gruen)

Underground before them, New York Dolls compositions (most written by Johansen) were based on a three- or four-chord structure. "Personality Crisis" (1973) for instance uses only three guitar chords: C, D, and G. The beat is a persistent, simplistic 4/4. Frequent equipment failures during performances (Kirby 1974, 41; Erlich 1973, 48; Simels 1974, 56) further added to the group's amateur sound. The band maintained this unpolished quality on their records as well. For instance, studio mixing for their first album, *The New York Dolls*, was so minimal that it took less than six hours to complete (Nelson 1975, 130). Paul Nelson, in a 1975 *Village Voice* article, described the New York Dolls' technical style:

> Their notions of technique mirrored more the tough sparseness of Hammett, the avant-garde fragmentation of Burroughs, and the cruel inward-eye of Nathanael West than the easy flow of media favorites. (26 May 1975, 130)

John Rockwell described the band's overall look and sound in *The Rolling Stone Illustrated History of Rock & Roll:*

> In the heyday of glitter rock, they were most striking at first for their looks—deliberately, poutingly androgynous. The band combined David Johansen's parodistic Mick Jagger imitation, punky snarl and ebullient energy with lurching [musical] violence from Johnny Thunders and desperately semiprofessional work from the rhythm section, and forged them into a music both barely controlled and wildly exhilarating. They reaffirmed the Velvet Underground's commitment to amateurish primitivism, but proved it could be energetic, dizzying fun and streethard all at once. Ahead of their time, loved within New York but hated or ignored without, the Dolls stood as a proud contradiction to all that was soft and safe in the commercial rock of the day. (Miller, 1976, 419)

Lyrically the New York Dolls were not of seminal importance in laying the groundwork of punk. Although some of their songs did contain a degree of pessimism (e.g., "Personality Crisis" and "Babylon"), others dealt with optimistic boy-meets-girl themes (e.g., "Looking for a Kiss" and "Vietnamese Baby"). Of greater significance in foreshadowing punk style was the band's vocal delivery: manic screaming which at times made the lyrics unintelligible.

From October 1972 to December 1974, the New York Dolls continued to play small New York clubs (the Mercer Arts Center, Max's Kansas City, and Club 82), toured the United States and Europe and released two albums: *The New York Dolls* (1973) and *Too Much Too Soon* (1974). Although the band amassed an enthusiastic following in New York among underground-rock fans, they failed to generate a large national or international following. Record sales, therefore, were low by music industry standards.[6] The lack of interest in the New York Dolls outside the relatively small community of New York underground rock was primarily due to the band's amateur sound and unwholesome image. While the underground-rock circuit in New York was rapidly gaining momentum as a genre which prized such departures from commercial trends, these elements of the New York Dolls' sensibility were not appealing to mainstream popular music audiences.

The New York Dolls' defiant behavior offstage contributed to the unwholesome image that they projected. The band members, all from working-class backgrounds and all, with the exception of Sylvain, high-school dropouts, presented themselves as tough, obnoxious, and streetwise. Their profane language, working-class accents, and arrogant attitudes became important elements of their style. Bob and Nadya Gruen's film *The New York Dolls: Lookin' for a Kiss* (1973) contains interviews with the band which clearly show their intentionally provocative stance. For instance, at one point Johansen explains how he intends to send the record company executives who are handling the band's album "a candy box full of shit, so they can just eat shit." Similar use of profane language and insulting statements is repeated throughout the film. Such behavior was sufficiently disturbing to mainstream audiences to impair seriously the band's chances of attaining a large national following.

The New York Dolls' association with alcohol and drug abuse also added to the band's degenerate image. In November 1972, Billy Murcia died of an alcohol and drug overdose (he was replaced by Jerry Nolan on drums). Thunders and Nolan were heroin addicts (Jordan 1986; Marsh 1977, 23; Palmer 1981, 17; Herman 1982, 74). Arthur Kane, a chronic alcoholic, was often too intoxicated to perform (Jordan 1986; Frame 1980, 27; Palmer 1981, 17). Patrick Taton, a Mercury Records employee who worked with the band in 1973, described his impression of the group in *The Village Voice:*

> The New York Dolls are one of the worst examples of untogetherness I have ever seen. Johansen is a very intelligent guy. Sylvain is really clever and nice, the others are quite kind in their own way; but put them all together . . . mix with alcohol, and shake, and you've got a careless, selfish, vicious, and totally disorganized gang of New York hooligans. (Nelson 1975, 131)

The band's interest in asserting a defiant and unsavory image disturbed not only mainstream audiences, but recording companies and booking agents as well. According to Paul Nelson, a rock critic who was closely associated with the band throughout their career, "Their destructiveness and unpunctuality alienated many promoters who no longer wanted to book them" (1975, 131). In 1974, after the release of their second and final album, *Too Much Too Soon,* Mercury Records dropped the New York Dolls from their label.

In October 1974, Malcolm McLaren arrived in New York from London and attempted to revive the New York Dolls' flagging career by becoming the band's manager. McLaren was a clothing designer and entrepeneur who, along with his partner Vivienne Westwood, ran a clothing shop at 430 King's Road in London. The shop, which opened in 1972, was first known as "Let It Rock" and then "Too Fast to Live, Too Young to Die." Catering to British teddy boys[7] and rockers,[8] the store carried an assortment of "drape jackets" (long, oversized coats); baggy, narrow-cuffed trousers; and crepe-soled shoes.

The New York Dolls met McLaren in London in the fall of 1973 when they visited his store, and maintained contact over the next year. According to Peter Jordan:

> The Dolls first met Malcolm buying clothes. When [the band] went into his store, they were dressed completely the opposite from what any self-respecting teddy boy or rocker would wear—from haircuts to shoes. Malcolm was impressed by the band . . . because the way the band was dressed—walking around the streets of London—was beyond anything he had ever seen. When Malcolm and Vivienne came to New York in early 1974 to show their clothes at a boutique show, they had a lot of things left and gave the band a lot of clothes. There was a nice rapport. (1986, interview)

When McLaren returned to New York in October 1974 for a seven-month visit, he offered to manage the New York Dolls.

Although McLaren had not been previously involved with rock music as a performer or manager, he had been closely associated with musicians who frequented his store and was interested in rock-and-roll fashion. In his capacity as the New York Dolls' manager, McLaren had more influence on the band's clothing and stage design than on their musical sensibility. For the performances given by the band under his management,[9] McLaren dressed them completely in red (vinyl pants, shirts, vests, ties, and high-heeled shoes), and used a flag with a hammer-and-sickle motif as a stage backdrop. Myles Palmer, in his book *New Wave Explosion,* explains:

> [McLaren] had always realized the crucial importance of visual style. He was keen on the Situationist politics of confrontation and controversy, and liked events and gestures which polarized attitudes. (1981, 17)

As with other elements of the New York Dolls' performance style, use of communist symbolism was not meant to be taken as a statement of the band's political philosophy but rather as a means to shock the general public (Jordan 1986, interview). However, this approach failed to interest even underground-rock audiences, who, in the mid-1970s, seemed to be more interested in breaking social taboos than in dabbling in international politics. According to Gruen (1986, interview) and Jordan (1986, interview) the New York Dolls' allusions to communism were largely responsible for the group's demise. Jordan explains:

The juxtaposition of red [clothing] and the communist flag was . . . ridiculous. It was meant as a joke. However, an amazing number of people took it seriously, including some of the groups' former managers. They didn't see the humor in the show. You had to be pretty thick not to realize that red patent leather suits and high-heeled shoes aren't exactly what they wear in Red China or the Soviet Union. That was a real setback. The band was dubbed as communist and people just weren't interested because they took it at face value. (1986, interview)

In April 1975, with no new recording contract, waning audience interest in the band, and management problems (Jordan 1986, interview), Thunders and Nolan left the New York Dolls to form a band called the Heartbreakers, and McLaren resigned as manager. Although Johansen kept the New York Dolls together with the remaining members (along with Tony Machine and Bobby Blain as replacements for Thunders and Nolan) until January 1977, the original impetus and vitality of the group were gone. The band did not record another album, and they ceased to produce new influences on rock style. For all practical purposes, the post-1975 New York Dolls, now referred to as the Dollettes (Gruen 1986; Jordan 1986; Frame 1980, 27), was an entirely different band.

McLaren's association with the band and his exposure to the thriving New York underground-rock community were crucial to the development of punk style. Returning to London in October 1975, McLaren became interested in revitalizing the London rock scene and subsequently masterminded the Sex Pistols. Peter Jordan explains:

In London there were all these kids who had nothing [in the rock world] to relate to. As they saw it, nothing exciting had happened in British rock since the '60s. There was a real gap. The energy had gone out of the good sixties bands like the Kinks and the Rolling Stones. There were bands like Mott the Hoople, but they weren't that unusual. Malcolm was impressed by what he saw happening in New York—all the new bands doing new and different things—and just put two and two together. [The Sex Pistols] was a great idea, and it worked. (1986, interview)

Jordan further explained in this interview that McLaren originally offered New York Dolls guitarist Sylvain Sylvain the position of lead singer with the Sex Pistols. Sylvain declined the offer. McLaren subsequently offered Richard Hell, bass player for the New York–based band Television, the position of lead singer with the Sex Pistols, and he likewise declined (Hell 1986, interview; Holmstrom 1986, interview). Eventually McLaren hired Londoner Johnny Rotten (see chap. 4).

Although the Sex Pistols personified a unique British rock style, the influences of the New York Dolls on the band and their fans are inescapable. Through McLaren, the Sex Pistols were introduced to the New York Dolls' consciously manipulated aesthetic of outrage. This included the New York Dolls' sexually ambiguous appearance, bizarre fashions, technical amateurish-

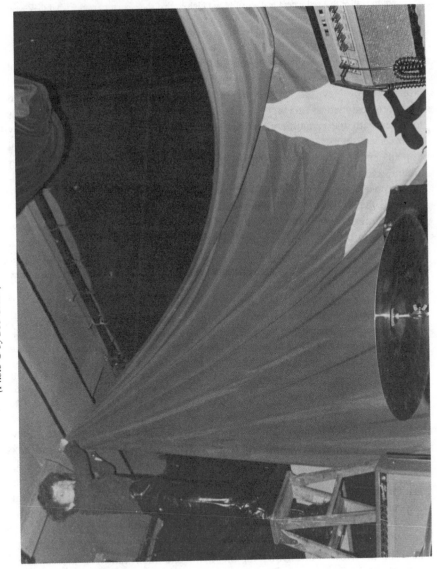

Figure 6. Malcolm McLaren Hanging a Hammer-and-Sickle Flag,
circa 1975
(Photo © by Bob Gruen)

ness, and antagonistic attitude. While these elements of style were not necessarily new to the world of rock-and-roll, glitter rock practitioners, and in particular the New York Dolls, expressed them to a degree that was unprecedented.

3

CBGB & OMFUG

CBGB & OMFUG, a small rock venue in Manhattan's East Village,[1] was an important catalyst in the evolution of punk rock. Opening in 1974 (and still in operation), the club provided a forum for unknown New York bands experimenting with musical styles outside the rock-and-roll mainstream. Although the late sixties and early seventies had seen the emergence of bands like the Velvet Underground and the New York Dolls, who challenged established notions of rock music, these groups worked for the most part as isolated entities rather than as members of a supportive network of like-minded artists. CBGB provided a home base for musicians and audiences interested in exploring new musical possibilities in rock-and-roll. The club atmosphere, rather than a particular band, became the focus of activity.

It was no coincidence that the burst of creative energy centered around CBGB occurred in the mid-1970s. During this time, the recording industry showed little interest in unproven musical styles, and few nightclubs booked bands without recording contracts. Unrecorded bands began to seek alternative performance venues, in search of an atmosphere conducive to their work.

The mid-1970s is noted among rock musicians and historians as a conservative period in the music industry. According to Janel Bladow, a freelance rock critic who closely followed the CBGB scene in the late 1970s and wrote the text for Mark Ivins' photographic documentary of CBGB entitled *Primal Punk,* the mid-1970s was

> a time of limbo for the music industry. Record companies, while signing new acts, were exercising caution rather than vision. Few were willing to risk money on unproven talent or new musical styles. Acts that were signed were musical, and often visual, clones of company artists with proven record sales. Hype and promotion were the keys to success, or so the bottom-line accountants thought. It was a time of "super" groups and stadium concerts. (1982, 1)

James Wolcott explained in a 1975 *Village Voice* article:

What's changed is the nature of the impulse to create rock. No longer revolutionary—i.e., the transformation of oneself and society—but conservative; to carry on the rock tradition. To borrow from Eliot, a rocker now needs an historical sense; he performs "not merely with his own generation in his bones" but with the knowledge that all of pop culture forms a "simultaneous order." The landscape is no longer virginal—markers and tracks have been left by, among others, Elvis, Buddy Holly, Chuck Berry, and the Beatles—and it exists not to be transformed but cultivated. (1975, 6)

In New York in the 1970s, there was no lack of rock musicians with new ideas and a desire to explore new approaches to the rock idiom—to produce a musical style unique to their generation. The difficulty in finding appropriate performance spaces inhibited their development. For instance, The Bottom Line, Manhattan's foremost mainstream rock club, required that bands be signed to a major record label in order to secure bookings. The same was true for the Palladium, the Beacon Theatre, and other thriving rock venues of the period. Ira Mayer, in a 1974 *Village Voice* article, described the then-recent demise of several small New York rock clubs, including the Bitter End, Kenny's Castaways, and the Metro. According to Mayer, this was due to the fact that mainstream clubs had "virtually monopolized the support of that $2-billion-a-year monolith, the record industry. . . . A New York club cannot exist without that support" (1974, 58). Mayer goes on to explain, in the case of the Bottom Line, the advantages of recording industry support:

Although the Bottom Line purchases a certain number of spots on WNEW-FM (and occasionally other stations) to announce its line-up, record companies supplement those ads with special commercials for their acts, usually tied in to recent products. Another source of revenue is the press parties for press, record company employees, and the rack jobbers and distributors who actually get the goods into the stores. Finally, record companies purchase tickets for individual shows and provide guest checks entitling bearers to food and/or drink. (Among lower echelon press a full tab has become a status symbol. Some writers exist on them.) (1974, 59)

Clubs which did offer unrecorded bands an opportunity to perform often limited their choice of artists to those with a narrowly defined musical style which emphasized the theme of the club. For instance, Folk City dedicated itself, naturally, to folk music. The Lone Star Café became famous as a showplace for country-and-western bands who might otherwise have had difficulty appearing in New York City. Although not absolutely rigid in their choice of performers, neither club was willing to engage underground-rock bands.

Between 1972 and 1974 only three New York clubs regularly booked underground-rock bands: Max's Kansas City, Club 82, and the Mercer Arts Center. The New York Dolls, Television, and Wayne County, among others, were booked along with acts such as poetry readings, female impersonators, and comedians. It was not until 1974, with the opening of CBGB, that a venue solely dedicated to underground rock was available to musicians on a regular basis.

In 1973, the building which housed the Broadway Central Hotel was condemned and the Mercer Arts Center closed. The following it had attracted dispersed. According to Steven Hager, author of *Art after Midnight,* and an avid follower of New York underground rock in the 1970s:

> That left only Club 82, a hangout for transvestites and glitter bands at Second Avenue and West Forth Street, and Max's Kansas City, the original home of the Velvet Underground. The rock scene seemed to be dying and bands were getting desperate for new venues. Under the circumstances, even a seedy bar on Skid Row[2] seemed appealing. (1986, 2)

In March of 1974, Hilly Kristal reopened his bar at 315 Bowery, previously called Kristal's and frequented by motorcycle gangs, and named it CBGB & OMFUG, standing for Country Blue Grass, Blues and Other Music for Uplifting Gormandizers. According to Kristal:

> I opened the bar [on the Bowery] in 1969. Then in 1973 I opened a club called Hilly's on Thirteenth Street and started doing country music there. I couldn't maintain both clubs, so I closed [the Bowery bar] for a year. When I reopened as CBGB in 1974, I intended to do country music here . . . but I found that there weren't enough really wonderful things around within the country scene, at least in this area, so I started mixing it up with rock and jazz. (1986, interview)

The eclectic nature of CBGB entertainment at that time is exemplified by a series of concerts which took place from 14–18 April 1974 and which included an assortment of jazz, rock, bluegrass, and country western bands.

In March 1974, Terry Ork, manager of a New York band named Television, approached Kristal about the possibility of the band playing at CBGB. Kristal continues:

> Terry said he had a band he believed in and they needed a place to play. He said he would get a lot of people in, and so they played every Sunday for a few weeks. Terry put other groups in with Television, like the Stillettoes and the Ramones. He got all these other groups to reinforce it, and we charged just one dollar to get in. That was cheap entertainment—even in those days. It was quite minimal at first—just a few bands. Gradually as more rock groups who were doing their own music started coming around—groups that had no other place to play—I started to book more of them, and make [CBGB] exclusively this kind of music. Then I made a policy that the only way they could play here was to do their own music. Since CBGB was the only place these bands had to play, they encouraged each other and kept the enthusiasm going. (1986, interview)

CBGB is located on the Bowery in a section of Manhattan known as the East Village. The Bowery is a street famous for its biker bars, flophouses,

Figure 7.   Hilly Kristal, Owner of CBGB, New York, circa 1978
(Photo © by Mark Ivins)

winos, and drug dealers. Steven Hager, who frequently attended CBGB concerts in the late 1970s, describes the neighborhood:

> Not too many people were coming down to the East Village in those days. Overrun by heroin addicts and drug dealers in the mid-sixties, the neighborhood was scarred by endless rows of abandoned tenement buildings—many of which had been torched and gutted, and were now converted by addicts into "shooting galleries." The European immigrants and bohemians who had previously lent the community a cultured, Old World aura had been displaced by impoverished blacks and Hispanics. It was a dangerous place for white kids from the suburbs to be hanging out, but it also had the cheapest apartments in the city—which made it a haven for starving rock musicians, many of whom began congregating at CBGB. (1986, 3)

Kristal explains:

> Living was cheap in the East Village in the mid seventies. It was the end of the hippie era and just before the end of the Vietnam war, and things were changing. Rock music was undergoing a kind of renaissance, and there was a need for an affordable place where musicians could get together. People could live in the East Village for $75.00 a month. Now prices here are ridiculous, people just can't afford it—but then things were different. (1986, interview)

The one dollar admission charge made CBGB easily affordable for underground musicians and their fans, and was a factor in building a consistent audience for the new music.

The physical environment of CBGB reflected the needs of this group of aspiring musicians. It provided an intimate, affordable space which allowed freedom of movement of the audience; close proximity to and interaction with the performers; and a place that the new movement could call home. This was a far cry from what was by then a traditionally distant physical relationship maintained between performers and their audiences at rock concerts. CBGB offered a chance to be close to, and even interact with, the performers. The fact that band members mingled with the audience before and after a set, and watched other groups, was an exciting and vital part of the event.

Musically, experimentation was more important at CBGB than technical polish or adherence to an established style. Musicians and audiences at CBGB shared a common desire to explore new musical styles, but the CBGB sound was not homogeneous. Each band had its own particular style, from Richard Hell's dissonant compositions, to Patti Smith's beat poetry, to the Ramones' fast, furious 4/4 aural assault.

According to *The Rolling Stone Encyclopedia of Rock & Roll:*

> Richard Hell led one of the most harshly uncompromising bands on New York's late-seventies punk scene, playing songs with dissonant, jagged guitar lines and dark free-association imagery that owed something to . . . the Velvet Underground. Hell had played with Johnny Thunders' [formerly of the New York Dolls] Heartbreakers and with the Neon Boys, who later

Figure 8. Entrance to CBGB, circa 1977
(Photo © by Mark Ivins)

became Television; then he formed the Voidoids to perform his own songs. They were regular attractions at punk showcase CBGB. Although Hell performed frequently, he remained obscure outside New York and London. (Pareles and Romanowski 1983, 249)

Richard Hell is best known for his song "(I Belong to) The Blank Generation" (1977). Unfortunately sheet music for this song has never been published (nor has sheet music for any other song by Hell), though lyrics for the chorus and first verse are decipherable from the independently produced single (1977). These lyrics are:

(I Belong to) The Blank Generation

I was saying let me out of here
Before I was even born
It's such a gamble when you've got a face
It's a facination to observe what the mirror does
But when I dine it's for the wall
That I set a place

I belong to the blank generation
And I can take it or leave it each time
I belong to the —— generation
And I can take it or leave it each time
(Chorus)

According to Bladow:

With the stark image it projected, the music that would come to be known as Punk acquired a negative reputation, which was not altogether unjustified. Its credo, "Live fast, die young, leave a good-looking corpse," was at times repeated only half jokingly. The "Blank Generation"—so described in a song of the same name by Richard Hell and the Voidoids—was born. (1982, 5)

Hell was also noted for his unusual clothing. Showing up for performances at CBGB in torn T-shirts held together with safety pins, his rebellious attitude toward bourgeois society went beyond lyrical content. As we shall see later in this chapter and in chapter 4, this fashion aesthetic anticipated punk style. The fact that Hell was influenced by the Velvet Underground (Hell 1986, interview; Pareles and Romanowski 1983, 3) and was later associated with members of the New York Dolls via the formation of the Heartbreakers (which included ex–New York Dolls Jerry Nolan and Johnny Thunders) also establishes him as a direct link between New York underground rock and British punk rock.

Patti Smith was already known to underground-rock audiences and experimental writers in New York by the time she began performing at CBGB in 1974. *The Rolling Stone Encyclopedia of Rock & Roll* explains:

Figure 9.   Richard Hell, circa 1976
(Photo © by Mark Ivins)

In the early seventies painter-turned-poet and sometime playwright (*Cowboy Mouth*, with Sam Shepard) Patti Smith began to set her poems[3] to the electric guitar backup of rock critic Lenny Kaye. By the end of the decade, she had proved remarkably influential, releasing what may be the first punk-rock record (the independent single "Hey Joe" b/w "Piss Factory," 1974). Along with Television she helped put New York's punk-rock landmark CBGB on the map. (Pareles and Romanowski 1983, 511)

At this time, Smith's song "Rock and Roll Nigger" (1976) is her only composition available in notated form. This score demonstrates the simplicity of her musical style. Utilizing only three guitar chords (E, D, and A), Smith's style is reminiscent of both the Velvet Underground (John Cale, former member of the Velvet Underground, produced Smith's first album *Horses* in 1975) and the New York Dolls, and is representative of the rudimentary compositional formats which have come to be associated with New York underground-rock bands.

The Ramones shared Smith's interest in simple musical compositions. Pareles and Romanowski describe the music of the Ramones as consisting of "simple but fast songs . . . no solos and a wall of guitar chords" (1983, 456). The amateur sound of Ramones songs was underscored by the band's aggressive performance style and lyrical content. According to James Wolcott in a 1975 *Village Voice* review entitled "Chord Killers," the Ramones

play with a chopping freneticism, the pace so brutal that the audience can barely catch its breath. A Ramones rampage is intoxicating—it's exciting to hear the voltage sizzle—but how long can they keep it up? Maybe that's why their sets average [only] twenty minutes. (21 July 1975, 96)

To my knowledge, no sheet music of original Ramones compositions has been published, though the chorus to "Now I Wanna Sniff Some Glue" is decipherable from their 1976 album *Ramones:*

Now I Wanna Sniff Some Glue

Now I wanna sniff some glue
Now I wanna have something to do
All the kids wanna sniff some glue
All the kids want something to do

Titles to other Ramones songs of this period give some indication of the anti-social subject matter employed by the band: "I Don't Wanna Walk Around with You" (1976), "I Don't Care" (1975), "Beat on the Brats" (1976), and "Blitzkrieg Bop" (1976).

Richard Hell, Patti Smith, and the Ramones were among the most influential musicians who played CBGB in the seminal period between 1974 and 1978.

Among the first to play CBGB under its new rock policy, they helped to build an audience for experimental rock music and establish the club as the focal point of the underground-rock movement in New York City. Though their styles were distinct, exemplifing the eclectic nature of the movement, the common denominators of their work—a pessimistic attitude expressed through lyrical content, and uncomplicated musical structures—clearly foreshadowed British punk musical style.

Despite the eclectic nature of CBGB musical style, the club did project a particular image in terms of dress. According to Pete Frame, who closely followed the New York underground-rock movement and documented it in his two volume work *Rock Family Trees:* "Image was usually glitter-backlash . . . jeans, T-shirts, leather jackets, ordinary" (1980, 27). Kristal explains that

> CBGB bands and audiences weren't style conscious in the way the glitter groups or the English punks were later on. The only style [at CBGB] was torn T-shirts and torn jeans. [People] just came as they were—the way kids in the East Village dressed then. What people think of as punk style—really dressing up with different color hair and all—started in the U.K. Even though CBGB is referred to as a punk club, there was never much of that fashion here. Richard Hell was probably the most unusual dresser at CBGB. He used to wear the same torn T-shirts as everybody else, but he pinned them together with safety pins. But still, compared with glitter and U.K. [style], it wasn't that outrageous. (1986, interview)

In the summer of 1975, CBGB mounted a rock festival in which more than forty bands performed during a four-week period—from 16 July to 3 August. In the 7 July edition of the *Village Voice*, Kristal sent out a call for auditions for the festival, which were held 7–8 July. After selecting what he considered to be the best forty bands out of the one hundred plus who auditioned, Kristal established the festival line-up and advertised it in the *Village Voice* as "CBGB Rock Festival: Top 40 New York Unrecorded Rock Talent." Throughout the festival, Kristal continued to advertise performances in the *Village Voice*. Kristal explained his reasons for organizing the festival:

> I had been booking unrecorded bands for over a year. Many of them were quite good, and the audiences thought so too. By the beginning of 1975, we were filling the house almost every night. So I realized that we didn't just have a group of kids here who just wanted a place to play, we had the beginnings of a real movement—a new kind of music. I thought they deserved more attention so I decided to do the festival. I waited until nothing else was going on to compete with us and scheduled the concert in mid-summer. (1986, interview)

The CBGB festival was a turning point in the history of underground rock. Not only was it the first rock festival to cater to unrecorded bands in New York City, it also inspired new bands to try their hand at composing and performing, and attracted the attention of a wider audience and subsequently the local press. In August 1975, the *Village Voice* ran a feature article on the CBGB festival

(Wolcott 1975, 6) which put CBGB on the map as the home of an important new trend in rock-and-roll. CBGB had become a showcase for unknown local bands who were experimenting with new musical concepts outside the rock mainstream.

Malcolm McLaren, former manager of the New York Dolls, was present at the 1975 CBGB festival. This proved to be a pivotal link between CBGB and the establishment of the English punk movement. According to rock chronicler Pete Frame in his book *Rock Family Trees:*

> McLaren . . . saw Hell (then in Television), was blown away by his short spiky hair, torn safety-pin held clothes, and couldn't-give-a-bugger demeanor, and demanded to take him to London. Hell refused—so McLaren borrowed his image. (1980, 29)

McLaren refused to be interviewed concerning the CBGB scene, his association with the New York Dolls, the New York underground-rock movement, or the Sex Pistols. People I interviewed who were closely associated with McLaren during this period unanimously agree that he was deeply influenced by his experiences in New York and that, were it not for his exposure to New York bands, the Sex Pistols, and subsequently the English punk-rock movement as we know it, might not have occurred. For example Peter Jordan, bass player for the New York Dolls during McLaren's tenure as manager, said in a 1986 interview:

> McLaren, being a very vital kind of person, is attracted to what he perceives as high energy. The New York Dolls, and later the CBGB scene, were definitely high energy. Something new was going on in New York in the seventies—something that those of us who were involved with knew (or hoped) would change the direction of rock music. . . . When Malcolm went back to London [in 1975], the New York influence was . . . important in his decision to form the Sex Pistols. He realized that nothing new was . . . going on in England, even though there were a lot of kids who wanted to do their own music. He gave them some guidance and support and got things over there moving. (1986, interview)

John Holmstrom, an acquaintance of McLaren and editor of *Punk* magazine, which chronicled the CBGB movement between 1976 and 1979, explained that:

> The genesis of the punk movement in England was all wrapped up with the New York [underground movement] and Malcolm McLaren. McLaren was in New York during the summer of 1975, which was when they had the big summer Rock Festival [at CBGB] with Talking Heads, the Ramones, Television, Duff Darts, Blondie. Those were . . . the groups that epitomized the new rock scene in New York. And Malcolm was here checking it all out. He saw Richard Hell [of Television] wearing a torn T-shirt with safety pins holding it together. Television had opened for the New York Dolls at a performance when Malcolm was their manager. The whole New York scene was very incestuous so [McLaren] was exposed to a lot of things all at once. Then Malcolm went back to England and started a band [the Sex Pistols] based on his shop, which was a clothing store that catered to rock musicians and their fans.

He got a lot of his ideas from the fashions he saw in New York, and also from the music—from the idea that it was possible to create a new scene and do a new kind of music that appealed to restless kids looking for something they could relate to. (1986, interview)

In January 1976, a new magazine called *Punk,* which was centered around the CBGB scene, appeared in New York. Published between January 1976 and August 1979,[4] the magazine was founded and edited by John Holmstrom, a twenty-two-year-old student of the School of Visual Arts in New York. While at the School of Visual Arts, Holmstrom studied cartoon art with Harvey Kurtzman (founder of *Mad Magazine*) and Will Eisner (founder of *The Spirit*—a newspaper comic book which began publication in 1945). Holmstrom describes the founding of *Punk* in this way:

Originally I wanted to be a freelance cartoonist, but I wasn't making it, and I ran out of money. I had always wanted to bring out my own publication. Underground comic books weren't happening at the time—they were fading out—so I could see an opening for a new kind of magazine. Then I ran into [Eddy] "Legs" McNeil and Ged Dunne, two friends of mine from high school. They were interested in the idea of making a magazine, so we pooled our money, about $3,000.00 between us, and started a magazine business.

I was influenced by all kinds of publications. Everything from *Creem* magazine to underground newspapers to French comic books. I wanted to jumble everything up and put out something interesting. Also, there has been a connection between rock-and-roll and comic books since the 1950s. In the fifties, juvenile delinquents read comic books and listened to rock-and-roll, so I figured I could bring that back.

I was interested in rock-and-roll, especially what was happening at CBGB. So we went to CBGB to do our first story on the Ramones and ran into Lou Reed and interviewed him. And then we had a magazine. We had a Lou Reed story and a Ramones story and we threw in a few other things and brought it out and just kept going from there. (1986, interview)

The first issue of *Punk* appeared 1 January 1976. This issue set the precedent for the publication's eclectic style, both in terms of content and graphic design. The *Punk* sensibility drew upon the varied interests of a generation which had not only grown up with rock-and-roll as a firmly established American phenomenon, but also, according to Hager, "had grown up on a diet of comic books, *Mad Magazine,* science fiction novels, illegal drugs, grade B horror films, and Saturday morning cartoon shows" (1986, 5). In the introduction to his book, Hager further explains that in the 1970s this "collective media-drenched consciousness . . . was dissected and rearranged, and eventually regurgitated into new forms" (1986, 1).

The content of the first issue of *Punk* reflects these varied interests and clearly shows the beginning of a process of self-conscious commentary on the heritage of the suburban American teenager. Issue One includes the aforementioned articles on Lou Reed and the Ramones, as well as a fictitous interview with Sluggo from the comic strip *Nancy,* an essay on Marlon Brando, an original autobiographical comic strip called *Joe* by John Holmstrom, a contest quiz, a do-it-yourself sixties protest song, and a "photo-comic strip" of Legs McNeil propositioning women. The magazine appealed to its audience as a unique statement of 1970s sensibilities, but it was anything but "authentic." *Punk* parodied life-styles and experiences common to middle-class American teenagers born in the 1950s.

The content of *Punk* magazine paralleled the lyrical content of such bands as the Velvet Underground, the New York Dolls, and the Ramones in that it contained subject matter and language considered offensive to the general public. Not only did *Punk* deal with topics generally considered unfit for middle-class consumption such as drug abuse and sexual deviancy, its articles were often delivered with a defiant nonconformist tone that included the liberal use of profane language. The editorial on page two of the first issue of *Punk* is a case in point. It is a direct attack on disco music, a mainstream musical style popular among young audiences in the mid-1970s:

> Death to disco shit! Long live the rock! Kill yourself. Jump off a fuckin' cliff. Drive nails into your head. Become a robot and join the staff at Disneyland. O.D. Anything. Just don't listen to discoshit. I've seen that canned crap take real live people and turn them into dogs! And vice versa. The epitome of all that's wrong with Western civilization is disco. (1976, 2)

Although *Punk* was structured on a standard magazine format—including interviews, reviews, essays, and paid advertisements—the graphic layout was unique. *Punk* included an assortment of photographs, cartoons, comic strips, and collages. Perhaps most striking, however, is the fact that the entire text was lettered by hand. According to Holmstrom:

> The hand lettering was done in order to save on typesetting costs, but it also gave the magazine the look of a comic book. That was important because we wanted to appeal to kids who were familiar with comics, but also shake up their sensibilities—to get them to look at seemingly mundane things in a new light. (1986, interview)

Punk magazine can be categorized as a fanzine. *Webster's New Universal Unabridged Dictionary* defines fanzine as "a magazine, usually produced by amateurs, devoted to a special-interest group, such as fans of science fiction or comic books" (1983). Holmstrom goes on to say:

> *Punk* was the first fanzine to cater to New York bands, but it was by no means the first rock-and-roll fanzine. Rock-and-roll fanzines have been around since the 1950s. Besides rock-and-roll . . . there are also fanzines about just about anything you can think of. There are fanzines for *Mad Magazine,* James Bond, race cars, collectable 1950s paperbacks about juvenile delinquents, science fiction movies, you name it. (1986, interview)

The circulation of *Punk* magazine's first issue was 3,000 copies, distributed in the New York area. By 1979, the last year of publication, the circulation had grown to 25,000 copies distributed internationally (United States, England, Australia) with a subscription list of 2,000. Daniel Lewis, who regularly attended concerts at CBGB between 1974 and 1978 explains the impact of *Punk* on New York underground-rock audiences:

> *Punk* was an important addition to the whole [CBGB] scene because it added a written forum to the performing forum. It expanded the audience beyond just the people who came to the concerts—in effect it was publicity for the bands. It also reinforced the ideas that the CBGB bands were interested in since it made fun of or rebelled against the status quo of middle-class America. It was like graffiti for us—it was our writing on the wall. (1986, interview)

Beginning with its first issue, *Punk* was imported to England by Rough Trade, a London-based distributing company which specialized in freelance American publications. By July 1976, with the fourth issue of *Punk*, Rough Trade was importing more than 3,000 copies of each issue to the London area. *Punk* quickly became popular among London rock audiences, particularly those interested in the recently formed Sex Pistols, and was responsible for spawning an interest in fanzines centered on the emerging British punk-rock scene. *Punk* also influenced the graphic sensibilities of these publications. Though the British punk movement elaborated upon the *Punk* graphic sensibility, the connections between the two are apparent (see chaps. 4 and 5).

In July 1976, the first fanzine catering to British punk-rock fans appeared in London, entitled *Sniffin' Glue*. Several months later a number of other British fanzines appeared, including *Ripped and Torn* (November 1976), *Rotten to the Core* (January 1977), *London's Burning* (January 1977), *Live Wire* (January 1977), *Vive la Résistance* (February 1977), and *Heat* (October 1977). Record charts, articles, and reviews printed in these fanzines clearly show the influence of New York-based bands on British punk-rock audiences. For instance, the October/November 1977 issue of *Heat* gives Richard Hell's *The Blank Generation* the number one album rating. *Ripped and Torn's* January 1977 record chart features a number of CBGB regulars, including Richard Hell, the Ramones, Patti Smith, and Blondie, as well as a poster of Lou Reed and Patti Smith. Albums by Patti Smith (*Radio Ethiopia* 1976) and Lou Reed (*Rock 'n' Roll Heart* 1976) are reviewed in the October 1976 issue of *Sniffin' Glue*.

The association of Malcolm McLaren with CBGB bands, and his subsequent involvement with the emerging punk-rock scene in Britain, particularly his work with the Sex Pistols, indicate a direct link between CBGB and the development of punk-rock style. The popularity of *Punk* magazine in Britain and references to underground-rock musicians in British fanzines corroborate this connection and document the shared musical and philosophical ideas of

New York underground rock and the punk-rock movement in Britain. The CBGB bands' interest in controversial subject matter and their unpolished, amateur sound were later elaborated upon by British punk rockers. By providing a forum for musicians producing original material outside the rock-and-roll mainstream, CBGB encouraged the development of a new kind of music which profoundly influenced the evolution of punk rock.

4

Crystallization of Punk Style: The Sex Pistols

According to American mythology, psychopaths and rock 'n' roll stars have almost invisible origins, springing parthenogenetically out of the headlines or onto the record charts as if they had no past.
Jim Miller, *The Rolling Stone Illustrated History of Rock & Roll*

In whichever category one considers the Sex Pistols, their story lends substance to the myth. They appeared seemingly out of nowhere to blast the rock world with a sound and a fury that was breathtaking. Their message was a mighty thumb of the nose to the cultural status quo of England in the 1970s, and it was delivered in raw, harsh terms. Mainstream rock culture, bourgeois society, Western civilization, history, the Beatles, and unemployment were just a few of the objects of their venom and contempt. They declared open rebellion on the ruling ideology of the times, all the "perceived-accepted-suffered cultural objects that ... act functionally on men via a process that escapes them" (Althusser 1969, cited by Hebdige 1979, 12), that is, the images, concepts and structures that unconsciously shape the thoughts and lives of society (ibid.). Teenage anger and alienation found a strident, booming voice in the Sex Pistols. Four strays, misfits, punks, with only a rudimentary understanding of music, thrown together by fortuitous accident, under the guidance of a clothing salesman, reared up from the anonymity of the streets of London and forced the world to take notice. Like the ingredients of a time bomb, they exploded onto the rock music scene in 1976, a savage counterpoint to the bland popular music then in vogue. Cultural terrorists, they used rude and violent methods to demand a reevaluation of values and a new awareness from their audience. This was not, however, merely one more invitation to man the barricades, to "tear down the walls," or fight in the streets. This was no idealistic plea for teenage revolution. There was no clarion call for a new social order and no utopian visions were offered. These were punks, not social activists, and their message was bleak. The Sex Pistols' music was a brutal outburst of hatred and despair. Face life as we see it, they cried—frustrating, meaningless, and ugly. Scream it out with us . . . "There's no future!"

The Sex Pistols, and the punk culture of which they were the most visible proponents, were a truly radical departure from the artistic and social mainstream of the 1970s, but they were not, as we have seen, by any means an isolated cultural aberration. Though as individuals they epitomized the faceless refuse of working-class London society, as a group they were the personification of cultural trends and philosophical currents that trace their origins to the very beginnings of rock music. They were the most conspicuous and outspoken nihilists of the rock idiom. Their passionate approach to their art set the Sex Pistols apart from their contemporaries in the rock world, and enabled them to transcend the three-chord tedium that is so characteristic of the punk genre. With a commitment and an intensity that often seemed demented, they transformed their stage appearances from mere music shows into theatrical events, subverting the conventions of concert and nightclub entertainment, at times going so far as to pose a threat to law and order. Never in the history of rock have the doctrines of anarchy and nihilism been preached with such urgency. As the definitive voice of the punk movement, the Sex Pistols had a decisive influence on the culture of their times. Moreover, as the physical and spiritual embodiment of the many negative elements that have always played an essential role in rock music—the rock star as "bad boy," rebel, misfit, outlaw, hedonist, social outcast—they expanded the limits of rock as theater and conceptual art and, in effect, created themselves as a work of art. As Nik Cohn says in *The Rolling Stone History of Rock & Roll:*

> The decisive element is nerve—how much, precisely, do we *dare*? If we have been invented originally as plain, dumb, insignificant, a loser, will we dare to reinvent ourselves as glamorous, blessed, heroic? If we are cast to obey, will we dare to command? And if we are doomed, will we at least dare to blow ourselves sky-high, in magnificent technorama wipeout, rather than drain away slowly, craven on our knees? (Miller, ed. 1980, 151)

The Sex Pistols accepted every dare. They represent a chapter in rock history that is, at least for the moment, the definitive word on rock music as antisocial behavior. They took the image of the rock "bad boy" to the extreme, reducing it in the end to its absurd conclusion.

Why did the punk phenomenon manifest itself when and where it did? Why Great Britain? Why 1976? And why did punk adopt the specific forms and styles that it did? To give definitive answers to these questions is necessarily to oversimplify the issues. To say that ingredients A, B, and C were present and therefore resulted in D will not suffice. Any study of history must take into account certain intangibles. The social historian is not permitted the luxury of neatly pigeonholing his or her subject matter and filing it away in the manner of, say, a physical scientist. In the development of a social movement like punk, ephemeral elements—accident, fate, luck, serendipity, the *zeitgeist* of the times, call it what you will—play a role that defies quantification. For our purposes, the establishment of scientific causality is unrealistic. We must be content with examining the facts and suggesting causality. It would be facile to state categorically that punk was a direct, logical, or necessary response by British youths to harsh economic conditions. The responses to poverty are as varied as the number of people who suffer from it. One person may turn to criminal behavior while his neighbor, under roughly the same economic circumstances, may be inspired to attain the office of Prime Minister. On the other hand, to ignore the obvious connections between the punk phenomenon and economic and social inequalities in Great Britain would be to deny the validity of the philosophical underpinnings of the movement. Punk in Britain was essentially a movement consisting of underprivileged working-class white youths. Many of them felt their social situation deeply and used the medium of punk to express their dissatisfaction. But punk was not an exclusive club made up of poor people interested in social rebellion. It was an artistic movement that attracted people from many walks of life for a variety of reasons. Pete Price, editor of *Heat,* a punk fanzine published in 1977, poignantly expresses this aspect of the punk phenomenon:[1]

One subject I've been thinking about for some time and arguin' about too is this "punk" elitism thing. All the crap about being unemployed, unable to play, ignorant, cliché, stuff like that.
How did it all begin? Why are people hiding their social backgrounds pretending their from poor families almost ashamed of their education, qualifications "only *true punks* are unemployed" is a typical one I hear—how can you have a job as well as be a punk rocker well if I didn't have a job,—and didn't have any money—I wouldn't be able to buy any punk records, now would I, and what would the supposed "dole-queue rockers" like the Pistols and the Clash do then, if their audience was so *poor;* their audience couldn't *afford* to buy their records, eh? It's a well known fact—by now, that there are *no* true-blue punk bands. The ideal stereo type punk exists only in people's minds. *All* the people I know who are into punk-rock are ordinary. It's their very ordinariness (hope I spelt that right) of them, and their lives, that makes them want punk. It gives them—and me—something reactionary—something to brighten up our bleak little lives. I want this in big letters: IT'S HARD TO BE MIDDLE-CLASS AND BE A PUNK it's a contradiction—right? Wrong. Being in my position, like most of my friends, it's really tough trying to explain to people—morons—that being middle class; just ordinary salt-of-the-earth sort, and being, into punk-rock as well, is not a contradiction, it's a reaction against this middle-class *ordinary* life I lead. It's being different from the general morass of people, it's sooo hard to get this simple message across thou: I mean, if I were poor, homeless and unemployed, sleeping in hovels & begging to survive, would I be a better "punk" then? (October/November 1977, 2)

Nevertheless, a study of the facts surrounding the rise of punk and an appreciation of the ambiance and milieu in which punk grew are worthwhile and informative. Likewise, my definitions of punk are useful, and necessary for the treatment of this subject, but not absolute. To say punk as a movement was dead with the break-up of the Sex Pistols in 1977 does not change the fact that to this day one can walk the streets of London and find individuals who look for all the world like the archetypal punk.

Great Britain in 1975 had one of its highest unemployment rates since World War II.[2] The steadily rising cost of living made economic progress difficult even for those who did have jobs.[3] Working-class white youths were hit particularly hard by the bleak economic situation. When they finished high school, if they did, they either could not find work or were doomed to jobs which they found unbearably boring and which offered no creative challenge and very little pay. In *The Sociology of Youth Culture and Youth Subcultures* Dick Brake says:

> When the lad reaches the factory there is no shock only recognition, because he is familiar with defeating boredom, time-wasting . . . because he learned these as real experiences of mediating alienation, at school. The result is typical working-class fatalism. (1980, 85)

This working-class fatalism often expresses itself as antibourgeois and anticapitalist. Brake explains:

> As youngsters have to deal with the contradiction of a push towards affluence, success and consumption, they also face the run-down of the local economy, and the increase of unemployment. The social structure is seen as run by employers and politicians who are seen as liars and exploiters. (1980, 83)

Mary Harron, writing for the *Village Voice,* links this grim socioeconomic situation with the emergence of the punk phenomenon:

> Unemployment in Great Britain has hit teenagers harder than any other group. According to the *New Statesman:* "The proportion of unemployed under-25s is likely to exceed 35 per cent in the New Year."[4] This summer thousands of 16-year-olds will leave school and go straight on the dole. The longer they go without work, the longer they go without training, and the less employable they become. Being on the dole means living with your parents and watching the wallpaper fade; $15 to $25 a week doesn't leave much for entertainment. This isn't suburban boredom—it's desperation. You can see why Richard Hell's song "(I Belong to) The Blank Generation" was seized as a new teenage anthem. (1977, 54)

We have seen in chapters 1–3 that punk drew heavily on the New York underground-rock scene for its initial musical inspiration and fashion aesthetic. However, the fact that punk proved to be essentially a white working-class phenonenon made it qualitatively different from its New York counterpart. The members of the New York underground-rock movement were primarily from middle-class backgrounds, and many were college educated. Musicians were often poor and/or unemployed, not because there was no alternative, not because it was impossible to find a job if necessary, but because they were dedicated to a kind of self-expression that resulted in musical styles which were not commercially viable. The New York underground music scene seems to have been primarily a function of middle-class boredom expressed in the form of artistic rebellion: art for art's sake. In Great Britain, on the other hand, musicians actually did have difficulty finding regular jobs to support themselves. Working-class style and demeanor were not affectations of a middle class looking for "kicks," or "slumming it," as it were, but an actual fact of life. For this reason British punk was not just music for music's sake, but contained a real social message. The music was concerned with working-class unrest. At times it was a cry of social and economic despair.

Both New York underground rockers and British punks derived an impetus for their music from a shared dissatisfaction with the state of mainstream rock-and-roll. The musical style and content of bands which had achieved notoriety in the 1960s no longer addressed current concerns. To the vanguard musical community of the 1970s, mainstream rock carried no meaningful message. The rock music industry appeared to be a paradigm of commercialized art, supporting a seemingly impenetrable recording industry dominated by a hierarchy of "superstars" with great wealth. Mainstream performers like the Rolling Stones and the Who had become increasingly inaccessible to their audiences. According to Brian James of the Damned, a London-based punk band:

> It must be really difficult, after you've been playing for ten years and you're used to like lush limousines and anything you want at the click of your fingers, to keep your mind back on the street, keep your head basic. We're talking for the kids, you know. We're playing to the kids—that's what rock 'n' roll's all about. (Anscombe and Blair 1978, 10)

Rusty of the Rich Kids, another 1970s London band, explains:

> I know this guy who lives down by me. He says he's never had so much fun. He's only 16 and he never really went to gigs before and he always wanted to. He could never afford to go and anyway he could never see the bands. He says he goes to about three a week now, 60 pence at the Marquee and he sees much better bands, straight in front of him, sweating hot atmosphere; good fun and he meets the bands and talks to them and they're all just ordinary people. (ibid.)

That social and economic unrest should manifest itself in the form of a youth subculture in Great Britain is not unusual. The youth of Britain have a tradition of forming themselves into loosely organized but distinct, easily identifiable groups that dates at least as far back as the 1950s. In 1954 a style of dressing that revolved around the wearing of Edwardian suits became popular among working-class white youths. Known as teds, or teddy boys, their look was meant to suggest the outlaw dandy, the American western gunfighter in a frock coat, the hero of American western film saloon shoot-outs. Steele-Perkins and Smith describe this fashion:

> Urban cowboys came to prominence in the Ted culture. At first Teds adopted the narrow tie, but soon the gambler's bootstring became the convention. The bootstring was held together with a medallion: death's heads, cross-bones skulls, eagles, dollars, and other images of America, miniature boots or holsters, and later, the swastika. Then there was the little cow's head, based on the skulls of long-dead Texas Longhorns which littered the Eastmancolor deserts. Teds were Britain's first mass-market existentialists. Anarchists and fast-livers, they acted out the desperado myth. (1979, 3)

The group lost popularity in the late 1950s, but as recently as 1976 a concert by Bill Haley and the Comets, one of rock's first heros, was sold out by middle-aged London teds, and their enthusiam for American rock nostalgia resulted in a riot at the New Victoria Theatre (Steele-Perkins and Smith 1979, 21).

The 1960s saw the rise of the mods and the rockers. The distinguishing feature of the mod ethos was the love of fine clothing, as typified by the Carnaby street fashions then in vogue. Hebdige says:

> Unlike the defiantly obtrusive teddy boys, the mods were more subtle and subdued in appearance: they wore apparently conservative suits in respectable colours, they were fastidiously neat and tidy. Hair was generally short and clean, and the mods preferred to maintain the stylish contours of an impeccable "French crew" with invisible lacquer rather than with the obvious grease favoured by the more overtly masculine rockers. (1979, 52)

Barnes goes on to explain:

> The Mod way of life consisted of total devotion to looking and being "cool." Spending practically all your money on clothes and all your after work hours in clubs and dance halls. (1979, 6)

The rockers, on the other hand, stressed a leather-jacketed, outlaw, motor-cycle-gang mode of appearance. Like the mods, the rockers had no clearly discernible political or philosophical reason for their existence. The rockers basically wanted to be, or appear to be, hoodlums. The two groups shared a general antipathy toward each other that occasionally erupted in violence (Barnes 1979, 127). Barnes describes this mutual antagonism in this manner:

> Mods thought Rockers were greasy, scruffy, uncouth, out of date, crude and boring idiots. A bunch of leather-clad louts and layabouts. Rockers thought Mods were weedy, dressed up, stuck up, sissified, poncey and effeminate nancies. A bunch of prissy little jerks. (1979, 126)

The skinheads were a group that evolved out of the mod culture in the mid-1960s and were still very much in evidence in Britain at the time of the punk phenomenon. They achieved a particularly sinister look by shaving their heads close to, and sometimes completely, bald. Knight describes their appearance in this manner:

> The young people who developed this style rejected the finery and the slightly effeminate characteristics of the art college mods and the hippies for clothes that were more related to their working-class background. They needed clothes that would not get torn in a fight, which would stay pressed and neat and which would identify them in a crowd. Donkey jackets, army greens, tough working jeans, industrial boots and braces fitted this need. Steel toecapped boots, highly polished, became a badge of identity and a useful weapon until they were banned at football matches. (1982, 10)

The skinheads were known to be prone to violence. Their antisocial attitude sometimes took the form of racism and even, among a "lunatic fringe," a flirtation with right-wing fascism and Nazism (Knight 1982, 29). They also were obsessed with their "Britishness" and were ardent nationalists. In general, however,

> most skinheads . . . couldn't care less about organized politics of any kind. Attitudes to parents, school and the police were not specifically skinhead, but like that of other working class youths. (Knight 1982, 33)

The punk phenomenon can be seen as an outgrowth of this tradition of youth subcultures in Great Britain. Each successive generation wished to define itself as being different from its predecessors. A major difference between punks and these earlier groups was that the punk style was more overtly political. Punk was not merely a fashion trend or a male brotherhood, but a social movement with, as we shall see, its own distinct philosophy.

Malcolm McLaren, clothing designer and entrepeneur, along with his partner Vivienne Westwood operated a clothing shop at 430 King's Road in Chelsea. As noted in chapter 2, the shop was popular among teddy boys and rockers. The shop was not just a commercial enterprise for McLaren—it was only marginally successful as a business—but also a way for him to channel his interest in rock culture and keep abreast of youth trends. Chris Salewicz, in the 1981 Special Edition of *Punk* magazine, illustrates this with the following recollection:

> One day in 1973, Malcolm was sitting in "Let It Rock," as his shop was then called, when he had a cathartic experience similar to the epiphany received by Saul on the road to Damascus: The New York Dolls walked in!
> "I'd never heard of them before," he told Nick Kent, "but they all trouped into the shop one day in their high-heeled shoes and I was very impressed by the way the way they handled

themselves. There were all these Teds 'anging around thinking what the hell are these geezers doing 'ere? But the Dolls didn't care at all. David (Johansen) just went ahead and tried on a drape jacket while Johnny (Thunders) was over by the juke box looking for some Eddie Cochran records. I was really taken aback. I must say that as far as I'm concerned they were *the* group—the *single* most important rock band.

"They were certainly the prime motivators behind what's happening now . . . with the Pistols and this whole new punk-rock scene." (April 1981, 7)

McLaren's management of the New York Dolls during the last months of their existence, and his ineffectual attempts to politicize them, have already been discussed in chapter 2. His appreciation of New York underground rock, particularly the CBGB scene, as a source of inspiration for British musicians was apparent from his unsuccessful attempts to import Sylvain Sylvain, and then Richard Hell, to London. Unable to graft New York underground rock onto the British music scene in this manner, he returned to London in October of 1975 and tried something new.

McLaren renamed his shop "Sex" before he finally settled several months later on "Seditionaries," and changed the emphasis of his designs. He drew upon cultural taboos as themes for his designs. Sadomasochistic clothing styles and fashion accoutrements that suggested fascism appeared in his boutique. This was not an attempt to attract a clientle of serious pornography consumers or neo-Nazis, but rather to create a kind of antifashion which he hoped would become popular with the local youth. The idea was to shock the general public, a pastime already popular with local working-class teenagers, and indeed an established tradition among post–World War II British subcultures. Jonh Ingham described the goods available at the shop in the large circulation British rock-and-roll magazine *Sounds:*

> At Sex you can choose from trousers with vinyl pockets and zips on the arse, outrageously oversized fall-apart sweaters, studded belts and wrist straps, anarchy shirts with hand painted stripes and Marx and swastika patches and CHAOS arm bands, and the Sex staple, T-shirts— printed with everything from the Cambridge rapist's mask to the naked young boy that is the Sex Pistols' logo—and of course, out and out bondage apparel. (1976, 22)

Julie Burchill and Tony Parsons, in their highly editorial version of punk history, *The Boy Looked at Johnny,* describe the designs:

> None of these clothes were either designed or worn to make the customer look alluring; on the contrary, the flagrant fashion in which the clothes used sex as an offensive weapon required a certain asexuality on the part of the wearer. They used sex not to entice but to horrify, the perfect expression of which was found in Jordan "Don't Call Me Pamela" Hook, the Sex salesgirl who wore cutaway-buttock plastic leotards with black suspender belt and thigh boots while striving to make her hair, face and body as puke-promotingly repulsive as possible. (1978, 30)

As "Sex" radicalized its apparel, and consequently its ambiance, it gradually became a hangout for people who could relate to the rebellious sentiments suggested by this fashion. Musicians frequented the shop, affording them an opportunity to meet like-minded artists and exchange musical and philosophical sentiments. The punk aesthetic began to evolve. These early punks reinforced each other's ideas through their adoption of these fashions and discussions which revealed their similar musical interests. The shop became a focus for activity which would later shift to nightclubs, such as the Roxy and later the Vortex, where bands associated with the shop and McLaren began to play.

McLaren's role in galvanizing the disparate elements of punk style into a movement is important. Caroline Coon describes McLaren and his influence in creating the atmosphere in which punk developed:

> Physically rather ethereal and unassuming, he was nevertheless possessed of boundless zeal. He became the Diaghilev of Punk. Upon his return [from New York] he set about making his vision of a rumbling, anarchic, energetic and noisy rock scene, the like of which hadn't been seen in Britain for ten years, a reality. This ambition, coupled with his sense of fun and adventure, made him the ideal person for aspiring musicians to approach. Their first contact with him was usually when they drifted into Sex to buy, or otherwise acquire, one of his infamous T-shirts. Malcolm would chat to anyone interesting, and if asked for advice he gave it. He seemed to have a canny knack of dealing with the practical details of rock, and as a no-strings-attached matchmaker, career guidance counsellor and creative critic, he was much in demand. He manages the Sex Pistols, but many bands including the Clash, the Damned, the Buzzcocks, and Siouxsie and the Banshees have benefited from his advice and encouragement. (1978, 3)

Greil Marcus, of the *Rolling Stone,* further explains:

> McLaren understood that rock-and-roll was the most important, perhaps the only kind of culture the young truly cared about; he understood that for the young everything else (fashion, slang, sexual styles) flowed from rock-and-roll, or was organized by it, or was validated by it—and that therefore rock-and-roll was not just the necessary first principle of any rock revolt, but that revolt's necessary first target. (Miller, ed. 1980, 451)

In the fall of 1975, Steve Jones (guitar), Paul Cook (drums), and Glenn Matlock (bass) began rehearsing as a trio in Hammersmith, a London suburb. They asked McLaren for assistance in finding a lead singer for the group. He introduced them to John Lydon, "a bored youth who hung about the shop and looked as if he might be a singer" (Boston 1978, 14). The audition, according to one account, consisted of Lydon singing along to Alice Cooper's "School's Out" on the jukebox in McLaren's shop (Palmer 1981, 17). According to Paul Cook:

> We thought, he's got what we want. Bit of a lunatic, a front man. That's what we was after: a front man who had definite ideas about what he wanted to do and he'd definitely got them. And we knew straight away. Even though he couldn't sing. We wasn't really interested in that 'cos we were still learning to play at the time. (Miller, ed. 1980, 451)

All four members of the Sex Pistols came from poor, working-class London suburbs. London, like New York, is a densely populated city where peoples of vastly divergent economic, educational, cultural, and social backgrounds coexist side by side. According to Coon:

> It's in London's suburbs where the contrast between the promise of a better future and the reality of the impoverished present is most glaringly obvious. Drab, Kafka-like working-class ghettos are a stone's throw not only from the wealth paraded on King's Road, but also from the heart of the banking captital of the world. It was after feeling particularly hostile of Chelsea's wealth and well-groomed finery that Johnny [Rotten] bought (or acquired) a brand new suit, shirt and tie. He took it home and slashed it to pieces. He pinned and stapled it together again. And then he wore it. (1978, 48)

Before channeling their energies into rock music, members of the Sex Pistols often expressed their hostility and alienation through criminal and anti-social behavior. All of the Sex Pistols had criminal records.[5] Sid Vicious (who joined the band in February 1977) was arrested at various times for assaulting policemen, criminal damage, possession of weapons, and auto theft. Steve Jones, an accomplished cat burgler, and the most frequently arrested of the Sex Pistols, had a police record that included breaking and entering, auto theft, vandalism, drunk and disorderly, and vagrancy. According to Myles Palmer, in *The New Wave Explosion:*

> Steve Jones was an illegitimate working-class hoodlum who was heavily into car stealing, and who had been sent to an approved school. With his mate Paul Cook he claims to have dismantled a drum kit from Hammersmith Palais and carried it out to a stolen mini-van. After that they pinched some amps and cymbals. Their larcenous acquisition of equipment reached its peak one night at the Hammersmith Odeon, where David Bowie was doing his last Ziggy Stardust shows; they sneaked in with their wire cutters and stole 13 microphones, . . . guitars and Mick Ronson's Sun amp. (Palmer 1981, 17)

Caroline Coon, who closely followed the Sex Pistols' career, quotes Rotten on the subject of his youth:

> We had nowhere to go. So what did we do? We threw bricks at passing cars. That's an old favorite. That's something you can do in the flats. I did all the usual things like nicking cars and that. But everybody does. It's just something to do. (1978, 55)[6]

McLaren encouraged the group to write original music about their own feelings and concerns (Palmer 1981, 17). Given their harsh backgrounds, the outcome was no surprise. Their songs were as violent and full of anger as they were. Though all Sex Pistols lyrics are credited to the entire group, Rotten was responsible for most of them (Palmer 1981, 17). "God Save the Queen" (1976) and "Anarchy in the U.K" (1976) clearly demonstrate the biting social commentary and rebellious nature of their songs:

God Save the Queen

God save the Queen
The fascist regime
It made you a moron
A potential H-bomb

God save the Queen
She ain't no human being
There is no future
In England's dreaming

No future, no future, no future for you

God save the Queen
We mean it man
We love our Queen
God says

God save the Queen
Tourists are money
And our figurehead is not what she seems
God save history
God save your mad parade
Lord God have mercy
All crimes are paid

When there's no future
How can there be sin
We're the flowers in the dustbin
We're the poison in your human machine
We're the future
Your future

God save the Queen
We mean it man
There is no future
No future for you
No future for me

Anarchy in the U.K.

I am an anti-Christ
I am an anarchist
Don't know what I want
But I know how to get it
I wanna destroy passers-by
'Cos I wanna be anarchy
No dog's body

Anarchy for the U.K.
It's coming sometime, maybe
Give the wrong time
Stop a traffic line
Your future dream
Is a shopping scheme
'Cos I wanna be anarchy in the city

Many ways to get what you want
I use the best
I use the rest
I use the N.M.E.
I use anarchy
'Cos I wanna be anarchy
It's the only way to be

Is it the M.P.L.A.?
Is it the U.D.A.?
Is it the I.R.A.?
I thought it was the U.K.
Just another country
Another council tenancy

And I wanna be anarchy
And I wanna be anarchy
Know what I mean?
And I wanna be an anarchist
Get pissed
Destroy

The Sex Pistols performed their music with their guitar amplifiers turned up to full volume. The sound, especially in a small, enclosed space, was deafening (Parsons 1986, 25; *No Its Not the Sun,* undated). The music emphasized an extremely fast, repetitive 4/4 rhythm. The melody was usually simple, sometimes consisting of only two or three notes. Lydon used the melodic line merely as a framework for his half-spoken, half-screamed style of delivery. The musical structure was uncomplicated, with repetitive verses linked by a guitar bridge.

Members of the band had little or no previous musical training, and their self-consciously amateur style and raw, hyperactive energy resulted in the cacophonous wall of sound that became a punk trademark.

In November of 1975 the Sex Pistols gave their first performance at St. Martin's Art College. Johnny Rotten, with his leering, hyperactive demeanor, spiky hair, and staring, saucer-eyed look was the most visually striking of the group. Coon describes the intensity of his stage appearance:

> Johnny, looking like a berserk convict starving and strung up on a wire hanger, poured forth a vitriolic stream of antagonizing lyrics, alienating large sections of the audience. (Coon 1978, 53)

The band's aggressive attitude and appearance, combined with the aural and emotional overload inherent in their music, made for a performance which was nothing less than an assault on the senses. Virginia Boston describes this first performance:

> Audiences might tolerate biting insult or crude social realism from a safe distance, but the Pistols played at close quarters on a low-level stage, without barriers. The audience could leave or pull the plugs out. The first gig lasted ten minutes and then the plugs were pulled. (1978, 14)

The Sex Pistols played their second job the next night at the Central School of Art. This time they were allowed to play a thirty-minute set before being asked to leave (Ingham, October 1976, 24).

In December the Sex Pistols played at a number of colleges in the London area by pretending to be the official opening band for another group which was booked there. Although they weren't paid for these performances (in most cases they were lucky to finish a set before being thrown out), it gave them the opportunity to play. At first, audiences were offended by the group and refused to listen to them. The band was undaunted, however, and when jeered by audiences, they jeered right back. Gradually, the nucleus of a cult following began to develop, and a small group began to follow the band from one performance to another. The persistence of these fans is noteworthy. Since the band rarely had an official engagement, news of performances was usually passed at the last minute by word of mouth. This passing of information at street level would later be developed through a network of small, homemade publications known as fanzines.[7]

The Sex Pistols' first important exposure came in February 1976 when they played at a party given by Andrew Logan. Palmer recalls that McLaren

> is acquainted with artist and socialite Andrew Logan, whose annual Alternative Miss World competition provides a freakish cabaret for the arty and decadent set; people who are fascinated by any kind of sub-Warhol scene. (Palmer 1981, 17)

Figure 10.   Johnny Rotten, circa 1976
(Photo © by Quartet Books)

Boston describes the performance:

> The Pistols burst into life, doing their utmost to assault and insult. Jordan, fashion forerunner of Punkdom—adorned in bondage and with face and hair luridly multi-coloured—ended the evening being stripped on stage by Johnny Rotten. (Boston 1978, 20)

The local press printed stories about the event describing the Sex Pistols as vulgar and untalented. The result was twofold. First, it gave the group a degree of notoriety which began to attract the attention of an irate public. Second, and much to the chagrin of the media, it attracted the interest of an even larger number of young fans.

In February 1976 the Sex Pistols played at the 100 Club, at 100 Oxford Street in London. Throughout February, March, and April the Sex Pistols played a number of jobs in London, most notably at the Marquee Club at 90 Wardour Street, from which they were banned for fighting onstage and brawling with the audience (Ingham, October 1976, 24). Other clubs played during this time included the Nashville, at 171 North End Road and the El Paradise (address unknown), a Soho strip club. Ingham describes a Sex Pistols' performance at the El Paradise in detail:

> The small, sleazoid El Paradise Club in soho is not one of the more obvious places for English rock to finally get to grips with the Seventies, but when you're trying to create the atmosphere of anarchy, rebellion and exclusiveness that's necessary as a breeding ground, what better place? Name a kid who will tell their parents they'll be home really late this Sunday because they're going to a strip club to see the Sex Pistols.
>
> The front is the customary facade of garish, flourescent lit plastic and enticing tit pix, gold flocked wallpaper and a life-size gold framed lovely beckoning you within.
>
> Conditioning expects one to go down a hall or some stairs, but the minute you turn the corner you're there. A small room 20 to 30 feet long, bare concrete floor, a bar at one end, three and a half rows of broken down cinema seats. (The other half seems to have been bodily ripped out.) It's an unexpected shocking sight at first, but after it gets comfortable the thought occurs that perhaps it's not sleazy enough. It needs more black paint peeling from the sweating walls, a stickier floor. The Sex Pistols . . . fill the minuscule, mirror backed stage barely able to move in front of their amps. They are loud, they are fast, they are energetic. They are great.
>
> Coming on like a Lockheed Starfighter is more important to them than virtuosity and sounding immaculate. This quartet has no time for a pretty song with a nice melody. (April 1976, 10)

After being banned from nearly every club they played (e.g., Marquee, Nashville), the band secured a Tuesday-night residency at the 100 Club during the summer of 1976. By this time the ranks of the Sex Pistols' following had greatly enlarged, and the audience began to shape the tone of performances as much as the band did. Fans began showing up at performances wearing outrageous attire: plastic trash bags, bondage wear (e.g., chains, dog collars, leashes, trousers strapped together at the knee), Nazi regalia, slashed clothing held together with safety pins, multicolored hair spiked up with Vaseline, lurid make-up, and, most shocking of all, safety pins worn through flesh—cheeks, lips, nostrils, and ears. White faces, blackened eyes, and painted-on fangs gave punks the look of the walking dead—an impression quite in keeping with the idea of "No Future." Uninterested in the traditional trappings of gender distinct fashions, their neutered, asexual appearance was also an important element of their fashion sensibility. Though many fans took pride in assembling their own outfits, much of the clothing came from the shelves of McLaren's shop, where the foundations of the style had been laid.

The McLaren-Westwood designs were elaborated upon, and punk fashion truly came into its own. Punk fashion was antifashion—anything that was ugly or offensive to the general public. It continued to draw on cultural sore points such as sadomasochism, gender confusion, and fascism. These designs however were not meant to be taken at face value. Swastikas, for instance, were not worn to indicate that punk was in agreement with fascist philosophy, but rather to remind society of the atrocities it permits (Hebdige 1979, 66; Holmstrom 1986, interview; Cox 1986, 27). Greil Marcus' interpretation is that

> punk toyed casually with Nazi imagery (raising the specter of youth fascism, and also implying that Britain's victory over Hitler had simply led to fascism by a different route). (Miller, ed. 1980, 454)

Punk fashion included attitude as well as clothing. The lean, hungry look, and the dialect and slang of lower-class urban Britons was mandatory. The demeanor also included looking threatening and capable of violence. According to Hebdige:

> In punk, alienation assumed an almost tangible quality. It gave itself up to the cameras in "blankness," the removal of expression (see any photograph of any punk group), the refusal to speak and be positioned. This trajectory—the solipsism, the neurosis, the cosmetic rage— had its origins in rock. (1979, 28)

Amphetamines helped in many cases to achieve the look. Burchill and Parsons suggest that

> the look of amphetamine psychosis became desirable when the mass of new-wave disciples fell in love with their mirror-image innovators The Sex Pistols . . . making it necessary for the less adventurous at least to *simulate* the appearance of sulphate snorters: cold, piercing stares, exaggerated black and white doe-eyes, blanched make-up, rabid speech and an aura of a capacity for ultra-violent aggression. (Burchill and Parsons 1978, 46)

Johnny Rotten, who was convicted for possession of amphetamines, was one of the many punks who captured this look.

Figure 11. Punk Fan, London, circa 1976
(Photo © by Quartet Books)

Figure 12.   Punk Fan, London, circa 1976
(Photo © by Quartet Books)

By the summer of 1976 it was obvious that the Sex Pistols' following was still rapidly growing. Symbols of identification were being selected and codified, creating a highly visible and easily identifiable population. By early summer the term "punk" had already been firmly established and was used by both practitioners and nonpractitioners to refer to this group.

Among the punk population information was exchanged through the street-level distribution of small publications called fanzines. The fanzines provided information about events and performances, as well as an alternative to mainstream criticism. Virginia Boston says that in *Sniffin' Glue*

> the kids spoke for themselves to themselves. The format was immediate and cheap. It seethed with crude, uninhibited energy. The circulation began with sixty copies and quicky increased into hundreds. The content was insulting, brazen, attacking, and as unrestrained as the Pistols themselves. It was the antithesis of the dull sterility propagated by the established music press. (Boston 1978, 14)

In addition to providing a network of philosophical exchange within the punk population, the fanzines were also instrumental in defining the punk graphic aesthetic. This graphic sensibility was not limited to fanzines, but was found on posters advertising performances, T-shirts, jackets, and later, record sleeves. Hebdige describes these graphics:

> Even the graphics and typography used on record covers and fanzines were homologous with punk's subterranean and anarchic style. The two typographic models were graffiti which was translated into a flowing "spray can" script, and the ransom note in which individual letters cut up from a variety of sources (newspapers, etc.) in different type faces were pasted together to form an anonymous message. The Sex Pistols' "God Save the Queen" sleeve (later turned into T-shirts, posters, etc.) for instance incorporated both styles: the roughly assembled legend was pasted across the Queen's eyes and mouth which were further disfigured by those black bars used in pulp detective magazines to conceal identity (i.e. they connotate crime or scandal). (Hebdige 1979, 112)

In September 1976 the Sex Pistols were the main attraction at the first punk festival sponsored by the 100 Club. The two-day affair also featured a number of other punk bands which had emerged in the wake of the Sex Pistols. Among them were the Damned, the Clash, Siouxsie and the Banshees, and the Subterraneans. By this time punks had become a high-profile, highly visible element of the London street scene. Their ranks had increased to the point that the line of fans waiting to enter the 100 Club for the festival stretched around the block.

It was during this festival that one of the most notorious, and unfortunate, incidents of the Sex Pistols' career occurred. On the last night, during the usual performer-audience provocation, a glass was thrown, missing the band but shattering against a wooden post, blinding an eighteen-year-old girl in one eye. The 100 Club banned all punk bands. This incident set in motion a barrage of

Figure 13.   Punk Fan, London, circa 1976
(Photo © by Quartet Books)

Figure 14.   Punk Fan, London, circa 1976
(Photo © by Quartet Books)

media attacks against punk which grossly misrepresented the ideology of the group. Coon recalls:

> The public was encouraged to hate punk rockers for their liberal use of four-letter words and anti-establishment opinions. More insidiously, punk emblems were misrepresented and the punk-rock movement falsely and irresponsibly aligned with fascism and the National Front.
> Certainly the basic stance of the movement is highly aggressive and emotionally intense. But the press failed to make any rational analysis of the aggression. Instead, the incidence of violence, taken out of context, was greatly exaggerated.
> The music press and the Sex Pistols themselves contributed to this misunderstanding. The first picture *Melody Maker* ever published of the Sex Pistols was a picture of a pub brawl. When the Damned spoke out against violence, *Melody Maker* chose to headline the article THE VIOLENT WORLD OF THE DAMNED—much to the band's distress. The *New Musical Express* gave front page coverage to a tragic, fatal stabbing at a concert in Dublin, branding it "a punk killing." (Coon 1978, 126)

The resulting publicity and rapidly growing subculture attracted the attention of a wary, but interested, music industry. The potential for lucrative business deals overshadowed corporate distaste for the music—and indeed the entire punk scene. In October of 1976 the Sex Pistols were offered a £40,000 recording contract with EMI records, one of the largest record labels in Great Britain (Coon 1977, 47; *Sounds,* 16 October 1976, 2). Though some fans accused the Sex Pistols of selling out to big business, Rotten insisted that their intent was not so much to make money as to reach the largest possible audience. They began recording, and on 26 November their first single, "Anarchy in the U.K.," was released.

On 1 December 1976 the Sex Pistols appeared on the "Today Show," a British prime-time family news and talk show hosted by Bill Grundy. This appearance was scheduled when Thames Television called EMI to book an interview with Queen, a well-known British rock group signed to the label. Queen was not available, so EMI suggested the Sex Pistols as a replacement, apparently hoping to promote the newly released "Anarchy in the U.K." The Sex Pistols' outrageous appearance and aggressive attitude, combined with Grundy's provocative questioning, made for an incident which received international attention.[8]

The next day the Sex Pistols made the headlines of nearly every British newspaper and the band was launched into international notoriety. For example, the headline of the *Daily Mirror* on 2 December read "THE FILTH AND THE FURY!" followed by "Uproar as viewers jam phones." Due to public outrage Grundy was suspended from appearing on Thames Television for two weeks; nineteen of the twenty-two dates on the Sex Pistols' upcoming tour were cancelled; packers at EMI's Hayes record factory refused to handle the "Anarchy in the U.K" record; and EMI announced the termination of its contract with the band, paying them a £20,000 severance fee (*The Daily Telegraph,* 4 December 1976, 3; *The Sun,* 4 December 1976, 2). "Anarchy in the U.K." was banned from British radio after only five plays. It nevertheless sold 55,000 copies and made the British pop music charts.

In February 1977 the Sex Pistols' bassist, Glen Matlock, left the band. He was replaced by Rotten's close friend John Beverly, a.k.a. Sid Vicious. Vicious became as visually prominent a performer as Rotten, and performances became more extreme. Vicious used masochism as a personal trademark, seeming to compete with Rotten for the most outrageous persona. Photos and film clips from this time show an aggressive, hyperactive Rotten countered by a bruised and blood-spattered Vicious—the result of wounds self-inflicted both before and during performances. The Sex Pistols were at their peak. Accounts (e.g., Coon 1977, 53; Boston 1978, 15) tell repeatedly of band members spitting, vomiting, leering, fighting, and swearing onstage. The audience was equally unrestrained. The policy of performer-audience provocation continued, and violence was an expected element of performances. Beer bottles, glasses, "permanently" affixed seating, and anything else available were hurled from both sides. The atmosphere during Sex Pistols performances was one of unleashed fury, emotional overload, and sensual assault. The energy level was awesome.

The pogo became the official dance at concerts. In keeping with the punk ideas of amateurishness and aggressive behavior, it consisted simply of jumping up and down and into other fans at a furious pace in a densely packed group. Anyone could do it. It required no skill—just fearlessness and enough manic energy to be knocked into from all sides for hours at a time. The crush of bodies in a small space, and the frenzied action (and interaction) of audience members, became a valued aspect of punk performance. Several years later in the United States—most notably in New York and Los Angeles—the pogo would evolve into a more aggressive form with a more deliberately injurous horizontal thrust spiked with acutely bent elbows and knees. This became known as the slam. The pogo, however, did have limits. No one was ever seriously injured.

In March 1977 A&M Records, another British recording industry giant, signed the Sex Pistols and announced the forthcoming release of their second single, "God Save the Queen." 1977 was the Queen's Jubilee Year, and the signing took place at a highly publicized ceremony held outside the gates of Buckingham Palace. Within a week, however, pressure from the press and other A&M musicians who protested sharing the label with the Sex Pistols pressed the company into cancelling both the contract and the release of the record. This time the band received a £75,000 severance fee. Though the Sex Pistols had come out ahead financially, they were still unable to get their records released, and few clubs were willing to book them. The band might have lapsed into obscurity if Virgin Records, a smaller, more experimental label, had not stepped in. Virgin signed the group in May and released "God Save the Queen" later that month, at the height of the Jubilee celebrations. The BBC banned the song within five days of its release, and commercial radio almost immediately followed suit. It nevertheless met with enormous popularity and made number one on nearly all the British music charts—even those of the BBC, which continued to ban it, marking its ascendance by blank spaces.

In order to celebrate the success of the record, the Sex Pistols gave a party aboard (fittingly) the "Queen Elizabeth," a party boat which cruises along the Thames river in London. When the boat passed the Houses of Parliament the band began playing "Anarchy in the U.K." at full volume. During the ensuing set a fight broke out between a photographer and a member of the audience. Once more the Sex Pistols and their punk following made the headlines, associated with violence and abhorrent behavior (Savage 1977, 1).

The Sex Pistols continued to receive wide coverage both in the British press and abroad. The publicity made them not only easily recognizable on London streets, but billed them as "public enemies." A series of violent assaults on band members ensued. In separate incidences Rotten was stabbed and Paul Cook severely beaten with an iron bar by local youths unsympathetic to the punk movement. Rotten hired a bodyguard, and the band was forced to play under assumed names (e.g., the Spots) in order to secure bookings and avoid physical attack.

In July the band's third single, "Pretty Vacant," was released by Virgin. Though the message was no less subversive in its pointed social commentary than "God Save the Queen," it spared the U.K. and its public figures specific reference. This is probably why the song was accepted by both the BBC and commercial radio. Though the Sex Pistols were no more palatable socially or artistically to the cultural mainstream, a growing fandom made the prospects for commercial exploitation too appealing to warrant their continued banishment from the airwaves. A performance of "Pretty Vacant" was filmed for the popular British television show "Top of the Pops," and the song, like its two predecessors, made the charts.

In October 1977 Virgin released the Sex Pistols' fourth single, "Holiday in the Sun," followed closely by their first album, *Never Mind the Bollocks, Here's the Sex Pistols*. Both records received considerable air play, and the album made number one in the British charts within a month.

The usual problems, however, persisted: bad press, cancelled engagements, legal difficulties. The poster advertising the album was deemed obscene by British authorities because it contained the word "bollocks," British slang for testicles. A number of record shops were prosecuted. In the first case charges were dropped when Professor James Kingsley, head of English Studies at Nottingham University, testified, defining bollocks as meaning "nonsense." Prosecutions continued, however, and Dicky Brenson, head of Virgin Records, was eventually fined on obscenity charges. An Edinburgh branch of Virgin Record shops received threatening phone calls concerning the poster, and, refusing to take it down, was subsequently vandalized. Major record outlets, including Boots, Woolworth's, and Smith's, refused to handle the album. The fact that it continued to sell despite these major obstacles is evidence of the size and persistence of the Sex Pistols' following.

Never Mind the Bollocks, Here's the Sex Pistols, which included the four previously released singles, was the first Sex Pistols recording issued in the United States. In January 1978, a nineteen-show American tour was launched after minor delays when U.S. customs temporarily denied band members visas because of their criminal records. The tour started in Atlanta, moved on to Memphis, worked itself through the deep south via Baton Rouge, continued through Dallas, San Antonio, Tulsa, and ended in San Francisco. American fans, eager to live up to the much publicized image of their British idols, did their homework and came to performances in full punk regalia and with volatile attitudes. According to Burchill and Parsons:

> Memphis saw 300 peevish ticket holders smash glass doors when they couldn't get in, while onstage Vicious performed his predictable party-trick of indulging in self-mutilation with a broken bottle. At Randy's Rodeo in Texas the pogoing rednecks were made to lay down their arms as they entered the auditorium, and when Sid teased them "All you cowboys are faggots!," bombarded the stage with beer cans and drove the bassist to pummel a front-row heckler's head with his guitar. In San Francisco two West Coast would-be punkettes tried to win Sid's heart by punching him full in the face and leaving him with a severely bloodied nose. (Burchill and Parsons 1978, 43)

Despite the enthusiasm of the American punk following, the Sex Pistols' tour met with mixed audience response and the American public was generally as appalled by the punk movement as its European counterparts.

The American tour was documented in *D.O.A.,* a feature-length film by director/producer Lech Kawalski. This is perhaps the finest visual documentation of the punk phenomenon in that it captures the unconstrained energy of live performances. In the film we see Rotten's manic style at its best, wide eyed, crazed, and screaming. Vicious is covered with blood, sometimes aloof and preoccupied with his bass, sometimes laughing and spitting on the audience. At one point we see him club a member of the audience with his instrument. The film includes all the elements which made up the punk performance experience: fashion, music, attitude, and audience-performer interaction.

The San Francisco performance marked the end of the Sex Pistols' career. After the show Rotten announced that he was leaving the band. Rumors of discontent between band members and between Rotten and McLaren had been brewing for some time. McLaren, who had been interested in making a film starring the Sex Pistols and directed by pornographic filmaker Russ Meyer (an enterprise which was ultimately abandoned by McLaren) had spent less and less time concentrating on band bookings. Vicious' increasing dependence on drugs (mainly heroin) and his self-destructive behavior exacerbated tensions within the band. Rotten was bored with playing the same songs for nearly two years, and felt that the heyday of the Sex Pistols was over.

The breakup of the Sex Pistols was timely, in light of the philosophy they had asserted throughout their career. Despite their rebelling against commercial success and complacency, they had almost become another band in that tradition. They seemed to be on their way to becoming "superstars." Though the tone of their music and their performance style were not (and would never be) mainstream, they had become predictable and to some degree accepted by the rock-and-roll establishment. John Rockwell described this paradox in the *New York Times* in February 1977:

> The break-up almost had to be, . . . partly because it reveals more clearly than ever the basic creative parodoxes behind punk's apparent nihilism. . . . If the Pistols failed—if their energies gradually flagged, if their commercial success in Britain trailed off, if they never really found more than a cult audience in this country—the whole impetus behind punk, its existence as the quintessence of the fast, furious and exciting, could have seemed hollow.
>
> Worse yet, if they had "succeeded," they would have had to betray everything they stood for. (Rockwell February 1978, sec. D, p. 5)

Immediately following the San Francisco performance the band members went their separate ways. Jones and Cook departed for Rio de Janeiro with McLaren, for a show he had scheduled there. Rotten and Vicious flew separately to New York. Vicious, true to form, overdosed during the flight and had to be carried off the plane and straight to a Jamaica, Queens hospital. In a telephone interview with Roberta Bayley, a writer for the New York–based *Punk* magazine, Vicious eerily predicted his own fate, saying he didn't think he would be alive in six months (Special Edition 1981, 40).

Rotten lay low for the next several months, dropping the alias Rotten and reverting to Lydon. In April he formed a new band in New York called Public Image, Limited, better known as P.I.L. Jones and Cook tried unsuccessfully to keep the Sex Pistols going, but without Rotten and Vicious the group lacked vitality and disbanded after only a few shows.

It was Vicious who stayed in the public eye. Following his move to New York with his girlfriend Nancy Spungen, the couple's addiction to heroin got them into ever-deepening trouble. Spungen, originally from Philadelphia, had a record of violent behavior and mental disturbance that dated from early childhood. She moved to London in the spring of 1976 because she was interested in the then-burgeoning punk movement (Spungen 1983). Spungen met Vicious and introduced him to heroin. Their self-destructive, often violent relationship had long been a point of contention with friends and members of the band. They took up residence in New York's Chelsea Hotel, well known for its counterculture tenants. Neighbors repeatedly called police to break up domestic distur-

Figure 15. Sid Vicious under Arrest for Murder, 1978
(Photo © by Mark Ivins)

bances between Spungen and Vicious. Though they continually pledged their love for one another in a kind of bid for attention as a celebrity couple, sadomasochistic behavior seems to have been a major element in their relationship.

On 12 October, 1978, Nancy Spungen was found stabbed to death in their Chelsea hotel room. Vicious was arrested and charged with second-degree murder, to which he pleaded innocent. He spent four days at Riker's Island prison undergoing heroin detoxification before he was released on $50,000 bond posted by Virgin Records. Before his case ever came to trial, and after several suicide attempts both in and out of jail, Vicious died of a heroin overdose on 3 February 1979.

Sid Vicious took punk to its literal extremes. To most members of the movement, violence and masochism were merely playful flirtations with public disdain. Aggressive behavior was limited to safety pin adornments, pogo dancing, liberal use of profane language, and a few scuffles with police. But to Vicious there were no limits. He died taking the punk slogan "No Future" at face value. His death graphically symbolized the physical and spiritual demise of punk.

No one will ever know exactly what happened in the Chelsea Hotel the night of Spungen's death, but the circumstances surrounding this tragedy served as a reminder of the difference between symbolic action and literal interpretation. Vicious was the exception rather than the rule. A generation of rebellious teenagers was not about to follow him into total self-destruction. Punk was over. Its following moved on.

5

Fanzines

The literature of the punk movement provides us with an opportunity to examine how the musicians and fans themselves thought and felt about the punk phenomenon while it was actually flourishing. The punk fanzines—publications devoted exclusively to topics of interest to punks, and generally related to the punk music scene—are particularly useful in this regard as they are among the few sources of primary written material available. They were direct, uncensored expressions of the punk sensibility, by punks and for punks, in effect, open letters shared by the members of the punk community. In style, content, graphics, and overall tone of writing, the fanzines present a mirror image of the punk lifestyle. The prototype American fanzine *Punk* and its symbiotic relationship with the New York underground-rock scene were discussed in chapter 3. The effect of *Punk* in publicizing and popularizing New York underground rock was pointed out, as well as its influence on the emergence of punk rock in Britain. As a written forum for the ideas and sensibilities of the CBGB music scene, it served to bring into focus and reinforce the aesthetics of New York underground rock. Chapter 4 investigated how the British fanzines played a similar role in the development of the British punk-rock movement. This chapter will compare the British fanzines to the American and show how each reflected the different styles of the two music environments. Representative examples of punk fanzines will be discussed with reference to their relationship to the punk movement as a whole. Throughout the fanzines we find recurring themes, characteristics specific to the punk movement, and these will be examined. As a unified body of work, the punk fanzines provide an overall view, a synthesis of the various elements—music, philosophy, aesthetics, and attitude—that make up the phenomenon of punk.

Concrete historical and economic data concerning the fanzines is difficult to acquire. As with other primary material generated by punk culture, the fanzines were intentionally ephemeral—they were meant to be read and then thrown away. Because of the punks' lack of interest in documenting their own history (see Preface), very few fanzines are still in existence. Moreover, many fanzines were unnumbered, undated, and anonymously written, making it impossible to locate writers and editors, and information concerning budgets, circulations, and life spans. Although the average life span of a fanzine was less than one year, exact dates of publication are impossible to verify since no records were kept by editors, and, with the exception of *Punk* magazine, entire runs of publications are not available.

Quotations from all fanzines have been cited verbatim with no attempt to correct typing errors, misspellings, or grammatical errors. Because pagination is often incorrect or nonexistent in the fanzines, page numbers have not been given as references to specific quotations.

The September 1976 issue of *Sniffin' Glue* is a typical example of a British punk fanzine. The deliberate crudity of the publication, as far as illustrations, type, quality of paper, staple binding, and overall appearance are immediately reminiscent of *Punk* magazine. The differences between the British and American styles, however, are apparent. The British punk fanzine is rougher, more spartan, and has more of a sense that it was thrown together overnight than its American counterpart. There is an obvious lack of concern for quality of any sort. The cover picture of Bryan James of the Damned performing before a backdrop painted graffiti-style with block letters reading "Damned" emphasizes the strident nihilism of the British punk aesthetic. While visually interesting, the picture is poorly reproduced, indicative of the casual, self-consciously amateurish approach to publishing taken by the fanzine's staff. Indeed we find that this is a landmark issue of *Sniffin' Glue* in that this third issue is the first one with any pictures at all, an event proudly announced on the editorial page. In contrast, graphics are a serious consideration to the publishers of *Punk,* and though the fanzine is put together in an ostensibly careless manner, the illustrations and photographs are done with obvious skill by trained artists.

The size and scope of *Sniffin' Glue* #3 (September 1976) are clearly not the equal of *Punk* #1 (January 1976). *Punk* #1 has roughly twice the number of pages as *Sniffin' Glue* #3 (seventeen as opposed to nine), and boasts more than double the number of staff members (thirteen versus five). *Punk* #1 has ten feature articles while *Sniffin' Glue* #3 has only four. Moreover, *Punk* #1 has two pages of paid advertisements, indicating that it was intended to be a viable commercial operation. *Sniffin' Glue* #3 has no advertising and it is doubtful that the cost of producing and distributing the publication could be recovered from the twenty-three pence cover price. This strongly suggests that communication for its own sake was the overriding impulse behind the publishing of *Sniffin' Glue.*

The content of the two fanzines suggests the differing interests and motivation between the American and British movements. *Punk* #1 is a more eclectic work. While the main focus is music (Lou Reed interview, Ramones article, *Metal Machine Music* review), there are three features devoted to humor (inter-

SNIFFIN' GLUE...
AND OTHER ROCK'N'ROLL HABITS,
FOR ~~PUNKS~~ GIRLS! ③ SEPTEMBER'76.

THE MAG THAT DOESN'T LIKE GIVING YOU'UP TO DATE'NEWS ON THE MUSIC SCENE.

THE DAMNED ✦ SEX PISTOLS **WITH** ✦ IGGY POP ✦

Figure 16.   Cover of *Sniffin' Glue*, No. 3, September 1976

view with Sluggo, "Cars and Girls," "Joe"), as well as a poem by Robert Romagnoli, and a discussion of Marlon Brando, subtitled "The Original Punk." This reflects the eclectic nature of the New York underground-rock movement. CBGB welcomed many different types of bands and encouraged experimentation in style (see chap. 3). The audience was in large part middle class and college educated, and their range of interests was varied. They expressed their antipathy toward popular culture in a variety of ways, including some outside the parameters of music. *Sniffin' Glue* #3, on the other hand, is entirely devoted to music. The four articles include an interview with the Damned, Sex Pistols gossip, a feature on Iggy and the Stooges, and punk record reviews. The white working-class youth that made up the main body of the British punk audience seem to have been essentially indifferent to expanding their horizons beyond the punk milieu. [The only exception is an awakening of political consciousness which increased as the punk movement developed and slowly crept into the vocabulary of the later punk fanzines.]

This disparity of interests between the American and British audiences remained fairly constant even as the fanzines' circulations grew and they became established fixtures in their respective music communities. By April 1976 *Punk* had expanded to forty-four pages with a staff of thirty-two. This third issue included an interview with underground cartoonist R. Crumb (famous for his work in the late 1960s and early 1970s, particularly Mr. Natural and Fritz the Cat). No fewer than nine features were devoted to humor of one sort or another. *Punk* had clearly found its stride as far as style and content, and was a carefully conceived and produced publication. The July 1977 issue of *Sniffin' Glue* (#11) shows similar growth and development. The fanzine had expanded to twenty-one pages and was produced by a staff of eleven. There are advertisements, hand-drawn illustrations, and even cartoon humor. Still, *Sniffin' Glue* #11 is almost entirely devoted to issues directly connected to the British punk scene, reflecting the homogeneity of its readership and their unflagging interest in punk music. The commitment to poor quality is still apparent, however, and the fanzine remains true to the ideals of the punk aesthetic.

The contrast between the American and British fanzines is informative and useful in defining the differences in style of New York underground rock and British punk. The fanzines, however, are of even more interest for what they tell us about the similarities between the two styles and the cohesiveness of punk culture in general. While great pains have been taken to distinguish between New York underground rock and British punk in order to document clearly the evolution of punk style, the fanzines remind us that the devotees of these two styles were essentially kindred spirits. They had more in common with each other than they did with the mainstream society or popular culture of either country. This idea of an international underground community of countercultural rebels, suggested by the similarities in music and dress, can be verified by the recurring themes found in the fanzines. I have already brought attention to the self-consciously amateurish style which is a trademark of fanzine literature, as it is of the punk aesthetic in general. The fanzines clearly project the ambivalent attitude with which punks approached their work, both in writing and in music. The punk mind-set presents us with a paradox. It combines a hatred of apathy and a sense of urgency concerning everything related to punk culture, with an acute awareness of sociopolitical impotence, a belief that actions were inconsequential, that improvement either of self or society was at best elusive and at worst utterly futile. This ambivalence had a profound effect on the manner in which punks presented themselves to each other and to the outside world. Self-effacement is a constant theme in the fanzines. It is expressed through a self-mockery that arises from the feelings of inner frustration of which so many punks speak. Not only are they angry at society and the political structure around them, the punks seem to be angry at themselves. Finally, and most significantly, the fanzines bear witness to the sense of community shared by punks. An atmosphere of camaraderie is pervasive throughout the fanzines, and it is this that helps us to understand the rationale behind the punk movement. Despite the anger, frustrations, and contradictions that were so instrumental in shaping punk behavior, the fanzines demonstrate that the punk lifestyle was also a source of entertainment and satisfaction for its practitioners. Like members of any exclusive club, punks enjoyed the company of their peers, gained strength from their shared values, and took pride in their unique countercultural movement.

The self-consciously amateurish approach to publishing so evident in the form of the fanzines is paralleled in the content. That this amateurish quality was deliberate, and to a certain degree, an end in itself, is readily ascertainable. The cover of *Sniffin' Glue* #3 describes this fanzine as "The Mag That *Doesn't* Like Giving You 'Up to Date' News on the Music Scene." The editorial on page one begins:

> 'Allo, this is the third issue and this is where we either get stale or really bowl you over. I don't like the mag . . . it should be fucking fantastic, but it's just cruisin' at the moment . . . it's not bad at all really! (September 1976)

The editorial page of *Sniffin' Glue* #4 (October 1976) clarifies this attitude toward the fanzine and its readership with an editorial poem:

> "SNIFFIN' GLUE . . . is the mag for you,
> Mark P's the editor and don't care a shit,
> Steve Mick's a writer, one of a class,
> And if you don't like the mag you can stick
>   it up you arse!"

SNIFFIN' GLUE...
AND OTHER ROCK'N' ROLL HABITS, FOR THE NEW-WAVE ! ④ OCT'76.

What,this isn't a joke.If you want something funny buy MAD.Anyway,this issue is priceless.

Figure 17.   Cover of *Sniffin' Glue*, No. 4, October 1976

The table of contents is prefaced with this remark: *"WHAT CRAP HAVE WE GOT THIS TIME?"* The editorial page concludes with the statement, "It's getting to the point when you (yes you readers, I'm talking to yer) actually like *SG.* Come on now, you alright?" The fanzine *Heat* #4 (October/November 1977) is unequivocal in this regard. The editorial page states:

> *We're Not a Professional Mag.* We don't do it for any money, we do it cos we love it, and for a laugh. We like to make fun of ourselves, and to make fools of others. OK?

Nowhere is the casual attitude of the fanzines more apparent than in the interviews with punk musicians. The interview with Lou Reed in *Punk* #1 is a prototypical punk music interview. It is characterized by rudeness, argumentativeness, ennui, and a profound disinterest in the subject matter by both interviewer and interviewee. The tone of the article is representative of a majority of subsequent punk fanzine interviews. The interview is titled "Lou Reed: Rock 'n' Roll Vegetable." The dialogue is interspersed with illustrations depicting Reed's ideas in cartoon form. When *Punk* assures Reed that "we're definitely unsophisticated," he responds, "Doesn't mean shit." The interview continues:

> *Punk*   What does an interview mean to you?
>
> *Lou*   *Nothing.* They don't mean *shit.* They do *not* sell records they don't mean shit and I don't fuckin' *care.* (January 1976)

Later, when questioned about his opinion of various rock musicians, particularly Bruce Springsteen, Reed states:

> *Lou*   He's a *shit*—what are you talking about what kind of stupid question is that?!
>
> *Punk*   O.K.
>
> *Lou*   I mean, do I ask *you* what you like? Why does anyone give a fuck what I like! *I* don't give a fuck what I like! (January 1976)

Johnny Rotten mirrors Lou Reed's conversational style in a short interview with Mark P. in *Sniffin' Glue* #3:

> *Sniffin' Glue*   Do you like shocking your audience?
>
> *Rotten*   Yes.
>
> *Sniffin' Glue*   Would you be dissapointed if the Pistols' audience became unshockable?

Figure 18.   Cover of *Heat*, No. 4, October/November 1977

Rotten   Well, I think that was a stupid question and you were stupid to ask it! (September 1976)

The interview with the Damned in *Sniffin' Glue* #3 offers us another view of the studied casualness characteristic of punk interviews. Lead guitarist Bryan James' first name is misspelled (as Brian) throughout the piece, and rather than retype, the editor merely makes note of the error and comments: "Is a pretty good bloke, that Brian (sic) is . . . he won't mind!" The drummer of the band, Rat Scabies (Chris Miller), admits to needing no practice on his instrument, and describes the band's sound as "get up off yer arse music!" The interviewer concludes the article by announcing:"Well I must say that was the biggest lump of crapy serious writing I've ever read. I promise it'll never happen again" (September 1976).

Punk #3 (April 1976) takes this amateur approach one step further in the interview with Richard Hell. Halfway through the conversation the interviewer, Legs McNeil, the so-called resident punk of *Punk* magazine, announces, "I'm getting really smashed. I'm really getting drunk. Are you?" Later he asks Hell, "How about if you interview me, you ask some stupid question." The interview deteriorates:

Legs   I got a question here for you um I mean if you had to eat at a Blimpie base every night would you do it?

Richard   I mean do you really think that's a question?

Legs   No but I'm too stoned to ask you anything else.

Richard   I think you better go back to interview school Legs.

Legs   What are we gonna talk about?
     . . . .

Richard   Go on.

Legs   I think I'm gonna pass out.

The interview concludes with this masterpiece of journalistic hubris:

Legs   I'm gonna throw up.

Richard   Go in there first okay?

Legs   Yeah, will you talk.

Richard   While your gone. No. I'll turn off the tape recorder. I might say a word or two but I'll wait till you're gone.

Legs   You talk.

Richard   Legs is gonna throw up. (April 1976)

The logical conclusion to this type of journalism, absurd, but at the same time humorous, and quintessentially "punk," can be found in the *Heat #4* interview with a band known as the Adverts. Obviously frustrated by the irascibility of this group, the interviewer asks, "Have you got anything to say?" A member of the band replies, "Ya! Why did you get me out of bed?" The interviewer later sums up his reaction to the band with this remark: "I would like to say that I personally regret having ever gone to talk to you lot" (October/November 1977).

As we study the fanzines it is important to remember that not everything the punks say can or should be taken at face value. Image-making is an integral part of rock culture, and in fanzine interviews the punks are given a prime opportunity to define themselves—their rock-star personas—for their public. Sometimes it is difficult to distinguish between the public image and the private person. Thus, when *Punk* magazine asks Lou Reed, "Were you ever not bored?," and he replies, "Uhhh . . . no" (*Punk #1*, January 1976), I believe this response should be taken with the proverbial grain of salt. Surely his claim to endless omnipresent boredom is an exaggeration. This is the same man who declares on the album cover notes of *Metal Machine Music* (1975), "My week beats your year." This ambivalence is endemic to punk musicians and punk culture in general. The punk-star persona borders on formula. Initially one establishes one's credentials as world-weary and antisocial, preferably a criminal or juvenile delinquent, and at the very least, a rebel contemptuous of authority. We have seen in chapter 4 how part of the punk glamour surrounding the Sex Pistols stemmed from their well-known, and in the case of Sid Vicious, extensive criminal records. In an interview with the Ramones in *Punk #3* Johnny Ramone, on the subject of his formative years in Forest Hills, Queens, claims:

We used to be vandals. We used to rip T.V.s off the roof . . . and throw em down into the street. We used to go around and throw rocks, bottles through peoples' windows . . . we'd play sick games too—steal the old lady's underwear or something? (April 1976)

In the same issue, in an interview with David Johansen of the New York Dolls, Johansen asserts that he was thrown out of high school "for being a moron." He goes on to explain that he got fed up with a particularly overbearing teacher, and "one day I just . . . kicked him in the balls . . . and then the whole class went crazy . . . and then the principal came up and dragged me away and then they kicked me out" (April 1976).

The association of the punk image with violence, evident from the style of dress and sound of the music, is reinforced by the interviews and articles in the fanzines. In the interview with the Clash in *Sniffin' Glue* #4 Steve Walsh asks: "Would you say your image is violent or suggestive of violence?" Band member Mick Jones replies, "It reflects our 'no nonsense' attitude, an attitude of not takin' too much shit" (October 1976). *Ripped and Torn* #2 (January 1977) features a contribution by someone known as "The Skid Kid," who recommends: "What we need is some music to get us rioting and fucking the government up!" In a discussion of the punk scene in *Sniffin' Glue* #11 Steve (no last name given) declares:

IF YOU WANNA FIGHT *UNITE* FIGHT BACK AT THE LIES, don't take it like any other minority group, show them and yourselves that you do mean what you say, suprise yerself Punk, hit back stop posing. (July 1977)

This glorification of violence affected by the punk community is, however, ambiguous. With the exception of a rare few, notably Sid Vicious, who as we have seen was not averse to slashing himself with a broken bottle onstage, most punks did not embrace violence for its own sake, and had a more rational approach to this type of behavior. A certain amount of rowdiness on the part of the musicians and audience was acceptable and in fact desirable. Rat Scabies asserts in *Sniffin' Glue* #11: "If they throw things its fair enough, you know? You get a reaction, if they like it. Good or bad . . . it's a reaction!" (January 1977). In describing a Damned concert at St. Albans he says, "Throwing beer and bottles, it was very good" (ibid.). In the *Sniffin' Glue* #4 interview with the Clash, Walsh asks: "What do you think of the aura of violence that surrounds the Pistols, I mean, it can easily get out of hand." Band member Joe Strummer (John Mellor) responds: "I think it's a healthy sign that people arn't going to sleep in the back row." Band member Mick Jones immediately qualifies this statement: "I think people have got to find out where their direction lies and channel their violence, into music or something creative" (October 1976). The following description of an incident at a Clash concert at Trinity concert in Dublin is an example of unchanneled, misdirected, antisocial behavior:

Some were spitting at Joe at the start. *"Stop spitting, I don't like it,"* he roars at them. "Don't you know it's old fashioned." One bloke though, kept at it and about mid-way through the set Joe leans out into the crowds of kids at the front and wallops him in the mush, *"GOTCHA."* (*Heat* #4, October/November 1977)

Figure 19. Cover of *Ripped & Torn*, No. 2, January 1977

The Ramones, in spite of their public pose of wildness and bravado, make no secret of the discomfort they experienced when confronted with an unruly crowd at a concert in Waterbury, Connecticut in June 1975:

Tommy   I just wanted to get off that stage!

Dee Dee   I was dodgin' a lot of them bottles—I saw some kid get up and he had a bottle! I didn't notice if he threw it or not 'cause I didn't even look . . . I thought you were thinkin' the same thing I was—*you know—let's get the hell offa here*! (*Punk* #3, April 1976)

Sniffin' Glue writer Steve Mick puts the punk association with violence in perspective in his editorial in *Sniffin' Glue* #4 in which he discusses the 100 Club incident (see chap. 4) and the public reaction to it:

Don't it make yer sick? All these bleedin' reporters holding up the bar saying, they were there, they saw it all. They're washed up and old. I mean, take all this sensationalism crap about violence and punk-rock. If you wasn't at the 100 Club Punk Fest. and you read all that shit in the press about fights, blood and bottles you would be scared shitless! Fuckin'ell what was Giovanni Dadamo talkin' about? It sounded more like a feeble description of the Battle Of Hastings, everybody thinks of murder and masacre whenever punk-rock's mentioned now!

Three beer glasses were thrown by some idiot—alright, that was bad—but that can happen and *does* happen at many "hippy" rock concerts. It's just stupid, that's what it is, to blow up the violence on punk-rock and so badly distort the truth! (October 1976)

In the final analysis violence, in attitude and behavior, is not so much a key to the punk personality as it is a symptom of a more serious malaise. Violence is but an expression of the inner frustration and spiritual emptiness which seems to be a fairly common complaint among punks. While the image of the tortured soul can be seen, like the image of the angry, violent punk rebel, as another building block in the creation of the punk persona, when we read the fanzines this aspect of the punk personality seems to ring true. This feeling of frustration is one of the driving impulses behind the creation of this particular style of music.

Rat Scabies' feelings on this matter are fairly typical:

Sniffin' Glue   What made you lot play?

Rat   Failed [school] . . . and I thought I'd get me own back. No, I dunno . . . I just like hitting things. To relieve that inner frustration! (*Sniffin' Glue* #3, September 1976)

The Clash echo this sentiment: "The alternative [to violence] is for people to vent their frustrations through music" (Jones, *Sniffin' Glue* #4, October 1976). The Ramones, in discussing their penchant for juvenile delinquency, admit:

THE STEVE MICK COLUMN... YEAH, SO WHAT! -MP

Don't it make yer sick?All these bleedin'reporters holding up the bar getting drunk saying,they were there,they saw it all.They're washed up and old.I mean, take all this sensationalism crap about violence and punk-rock.If you wasn't at the 100 Club Punk Fest.and you read all that shit in the press about fights,blood and bottles you would be scared shitless!Fuckin'ell what was Giovanni Dadamo talkin'about?It sounded more like a feeble description of the Battle Of Hastings,everybody thinks of murder and massacre whenever punk-rock's mentioned now!

Three beer glasses were thrown by some idiot-alright,that was bad-but that can happen and <u>does</u> happen at many 'hippy'rock concerts.It's just stupid ,that's what it is,to blow up the violence on punk-rock and so badly distort the truth!

US AND THEM.

Something is happening, like,when the Jam recently played Upstairs At Ronnie's disco.It seems that a member of the Wild Boys(a group currently rehearsing) got mouth-wacked by a Disco-kid'cause he was wearing a Swastika armband and got branded as a"burner of Jews".It seems that the non-new-wave fans,you know,the'footballs'and the 'discos'are turning against us'cause we're out of line,we're differant and they can't understand it.

It's a bit silly,ain't it? I mean,we don't wanna'cause no trouble,we want to enjoy ourselves-possin'and liggering, shades and glue,sneers and bored expressions are all part of it.Punks are not girls,if it comes to the crunch we'll have no option but to fight back and fight hard!But it's silly 'cause who would really wanna badly hurt any one?

It's nothing new though,I mean,mods vs.rockers,skinheads against hippys,same old thing,you know?

Anyway,hope you enjoy this issue,punks have been telling us we've got the best mag around.Well,of course we have 'cause we're broke,on the dole and live at home in boring council flats,so obviously we know what's goin'on!See you soon...

Steve Mick.

P.S:'ere,how comes that creep,Mark P.got his photo in SOUNDS and I didn't?Still...nicked his column this week,didn't I?Up yours,MP. Yati-Yati-Star!

YOUR FREE S.G. BADGE → 2

WHAT CRAP HAVE WE GOT THIS TIME?

Front-cover:Joe & Paul of the CLASH by Roco.

Page3-6:CLASH Interview by Steve Walsh.

    6:PATTI SMITH/LOUREED-new albums reviewed by Mark P.

    7:BUZZCOCKS by Steve Mick. JAM OUTDOORS by Mark P.

    8:SAINTS by Mark P.

    9:DR.FEELGOOD-newie reviewed by Rick SINGLES reviews by Mark P.   Brown.

   10:Pin-up No.2: **FEELGOODS.**

"SNIFFIN'GLUE...'is the mag for you,
Mark P's the editor and don't care a shit,
Steve Mick's a writer,one of a glass,
And if you don't like the mag you can stick
          it up you arse!"
Also sticking things in various places are;
Rick Brown(who's a fool for a banana)and
Steve Walsh(who's likewise for rolled-up
Jonathan Richman cover).

Special sneers to:Roco(CLASH photos)and all the other people I love dearly(you know who you are).

Address of the"most exciting mag ever"(my dad said that).

SG,
24 ROCHFORT HSE.,
GROVE ST.,
DEPTFORD,
LONDON,
SE8 3LX.

This mag is published by noone....well,what d'you except IPC or whatever it's called,I mean it's getting to the point when you(yes you readers,I'm talking to yer)actually like SG.Come on now,you alright?

Don't bother writing after back-issues'cause we ain't got none!I don't believe in old news,we gotta think ahead!

CUT IT OUT AND STICK IT ON A BADGE.

SNIFFIN' GLUE.

OR PIN IT ON

Figure 20.   Page 2 of *Sniffin' Glue*, No. 4, October 1976

"This is before our frustrations were all taken out in our music." The interviewer goes on to explain that

> [the Ramones] are *very loud*. And violent. They stop playing in the middle of songs, usually three times or more a night, yell at each other, have rave-ups onstage, and sometimes leave the stage in sheer *disgust, anger and frustration*!! (*Punk #3*, April 1976)

Richard Hell, in an interview with Legs McNeil in *Punk #3*, is slightly more articulate in describing his angst:

Richard   Basically I have one feeling.

Legs   Yeah?

Richard   And that's this little voice in my head saying . . . well I mean the one main feeling I have is the desire to get out of here. And any other feelings I have come from trying to analyse, you know, why I want to go away.

. . . .

Richard   See, I always feel uncomfortable and I just want to go away. Just walk out of the room. Its not going to any other place or any other sensation or anything like that, its just to get out of "here."

Legs   (Laughing) Do you feel like leaving now.

Richard   Yes, I always feel that way. I feel like just standing up and walking out of here.

Legs   Do you want to go?

Richard   I do but I've, I've adjusted to this feeling. (April 1976)

Hell's opinions on romantic love shed some light on these feelings of alienation and suggest that they are of complex origin:

Richard   I think love is sort of a con that you play on yourself. I think the whole conception of love is something that the previous generation invents to justify their having created you. You know I think the real reason children are born is because parents are so bored. They need a way . . .

Legs   They want to fuck.

Richard   No they don't want to fuck, they have children to amuse themselves. They're so bored, they don't have anything else to do so they have a child 'cause that will keep them busy for a while. Then, to justify to the kid, the reason he exists they tell him there is such a thing as love and that's where you come from because um, me and your daddy or me and your mommy were in *love* and that's why you exist. When actually it was because they were bored out of their minds.

Legs   Is that why your parents had you?

Richard   That's why everybodys parents have everybody. Without exception (laughs).

Legs   Are you glad you were born?

Richard   I have my doubts. (*Punk #*3, April 1976)

It is perhaps from sentiments such as these that the words to songs like "(I Belong to) The Blank Generation" (1976) arise (see chap. 3). On the editorial page of *Punk #*3 Peter Crowley sums up the relationship between frustration and punk expression:

> The key word—to me anyway—in the punk definition was "a beginner an inexperienced hand." Punk rock—any kid can pick up a guitar and become a rock 'n' roll star, despite or because of his lack of ability, talent, intelligence, limitations and/or potential, and usually does so out of frustration, hostility, a lot of nerve and a need for ego fulfilment. (April 1976)

If boredom and frustration are the enemies of punk peace of mind, punk music and culture are the means of conquering them. The only sin one can be guilty of in this scenario is lethargy or indifference to the cause. Mick Jones of the Clash addresses this issue in an interview with Steve Walsh in *Sniffin' Glue* #4:

Mick   The important thing is to encourage people to do things for themselves, think for themselves and stand up for what their rights are.

Steve   You hate apathy?

Mick   Oh, I fuckin' hate apathy but I hate ignorance more than anything.
. . . .

Steve   What do you think is wrong with people today?

Mick   They're apathetic . . . boring. (October 1976)

Mick Cash of the band 999 expresses this sentiment: "I just wish more people would get involved with the whole thing" (*Heat #*4, October/November 1977).

We have seen how punk bands encouraged rowdy behavior in their audiences, but at the same time were aware that there was a line between good-natured, high-spirited fun and senseless, destructive violence. The fanzines help us to penetrate the myths behind the apparent anarchy of punk performance. Firsthand descriptions of audience behavior at punk concerts appear in various fanzines and they afford us a glimpse of the reality of these events as well as an entertaining perspective on punk culture in general. Mary Harron gives us this portrait of an evening with the Ramones at CBGB:

Right now I am sitting by the stage where Joey Ramone has wrapped his tall langorous body and his long long hands around the microphone to deliver "the Blitzkreig Bop." The audience sits straight up in their chairs. "1, 2, 3, 4!" No smiling, no amiable jammin, no cute fifties nostalgia. It's more like sitting underneath Niagra Falls.

This is an outsider's view. I just want to make that clear. I knew that I was an outsider from the moment I walked into CBGB's because I kept falling over my high-heeled boots. People who knew were wearing sneakers. One of the *Punk* magazine editors explained: "We don't believe in love or any of that shit. We believe in making money and getting drunk."

Black leather jackets surface around the bar, but it's the girls by the bandstand who have the image. The one with the puff-sleeved angora sweater and the white lipstick, and her friend with the red razorcut bouffant hairdo, black leather and shades. The shades have a ribbon attached, so she looks like a homicidal librarian.

I go to the ladies room. "Hey, ugly—who does your makeup—Helen Keller?" (*Punk* #1, January 1976)

In *Sniffin' Glue* #3, Mark P. describes a typical Sex Pistols concert in this way:

Sex Pistols—Any club, any date.

I can't remember what really happened at the –club to be honest. By the time the Pistols made it on stage the place wasn't the same anymore. I mean, it wasn't the –club, it was the Sex Pistols' club!

The Sex Pistols are a force, you get that feeling from their audience—and it sticks in your mind. The clothes, the hair and even the atitude, of the audience has a direct link to the band. On a club level it's a wierd thing, even I've got cropped hair now, you just can't help getting into it! As the Pistols pounded out their "music" the image was in every corner of the club. Their sound is pure enegy, you can't describe it in stupid words—you've got to experience to understand. I just liggered in the tense atmosphere, posing, like the other punks (or were they?). You get that feeling at the Pistols' gigs that everyone's posing so they can't really be punks can they? Punks are carefree, and I mean completly . . . you know, like a football who kicks in someone's head and don't care a shit. Yer, the Pistols crowd are not punks, they're too vain. But what's wrong with that so am I. (September 1976)

This next review, of a Radiators concert at the Music Machine Club in Camden-town, is a classic example of fanzine reporting. The ambiguousness of punk writing, the difficulty in documenting punk social events, and the ephemeral nature of the punk scene in general are epitomized in this short, amusing, and no doubt well-intended report:

We got down there early, about 8:30. The gig wouldn't be starting till 10:30. The place is huge, stage about 20 feet off the floor. You wanna be good to create an atmosphere in this place. After a few gargles, the first band, the Crabs, comes on. They went down OK; they had their own fans there who pogo'd all over the place. Next came the New Hearts—real slick, the singer wore a red suit. As the sound was so bad, we couldn't make out much song titles. At the end they storm off very angry the drummer throws his sticks at the lights, and the singer throws the mike-stand down into the ground.

Finally, the Radiators hit the stage. Straight into "Television Screen" sounds as good as ever. At the night's end Chevron announced that Johnny Thunders was getting up to play with them! This woke up the posers! Thunders came on dressed totally in leathers . . . really cool lookin'. They went through "Psychotic Reaction" next came "T.V. Screen" much better:—Pete rolling all over the stage—great. Thunders was really enjoyin' it. Kept prowling around and doing his guitar hero pose. The set finished with what sounded like "Johnny B. Goode" to me, but I think everybody was playing something different.

The crowds in these places, thou; are only posers. They come in dressed to kill, but they never dance, maybe it's all that masochist gear hurting them, their not worth talkin' about. (*Heat* #4, October/November 1977)

Questions immediately arise. From this writing can we tell whether or not this was an enjoyable, successful evening of punk entertainment? More to the point, did this crowd like to dance, or didn't they? Whatever the case, this piece has an element of charm to it and in some ways tells us more about the atmosphere of a typical punk concert than an article with one hundred verifiable, documentable facts.

It is this aspect of the fanzines—that they offer an insider's view of the punk world—that makes them so valuable as a research tool for the historian. Fanzines are clearly not a strict chronicle of events concerning the punk movement. They were not intended to be. They give us, however, something equally important—a feeling for the atmosphere of the punk milieu. Moreover, they provide evidence of the strong sense of community shared by punks. The feeling of camaraderie characteristic of the punk movement is implicit in all the interviews and articles of the fanzines. The pervasive "us against them" attitude reinforces this sense of shared experience. The virulent attacks on the mainstream media, and rabid defense of their rock groups, music, and lifestyle bear witness to this. All of these elements are present in an article written by an anonymous fan in *Ripped and Torn* #2:

There was not one fucking paper with the guts to defend the Pistols in *any* way. My paranoid mind makes me think its a Big Brother type figure putting pressure to discredit punks, and we won't be pushed around and fobbed with phoney ideals. You cant watch T.V., listen to the radio, or read a paper nowadays without some . . . [body] slagging off the punk or the Pistols . . . I've gone on a bit I know, but theres so much "pure hatred" against punk, that I've got to do something. Just watch out for any restrictions, and keep on liking the music (we're the only free thinkers left) whatever happens. (January 1977)

The article concludes with this recommendation:

HATE THESE THINGS, OK!!

the Establishment, the Authorities, Apathy, compromise, complacency, Nostalgia, Led Zeppelin, E.L.P., Yes, Starsky and Hutch (and all police t.v. progs.), the media. (January 1977)

The sense of separation from mainstream culture and the exclusivity of the punk community is enhanced by record reviews found in the punk fanzines. Reviewers discuss songs like "Drano in Your Veins" and "Texas Chainsaw Massacre Boogie" (both songs undated) as though this is as normal as reviewing a cut from a Frank Sinatra album. The idea that membership in the punk community was predicated on shared musical tastes is evident from the following typical examples:

DAMNED—New Rose (Stiff).
  At last, a real "punk" single. The Damned, one of the hardest bands around, have come up with a killer. Produced by Nick Lowe, this single carries everything the Damned have to offer. The energy on "New Rose" is frightening, listen to this and realise what it's all about. Everyone, old musicians, old "stars," the British record-buying public—find out how rock should sound on record. Buy this thing or be very boring! (*Sniffin' Glue* #4, October 1976)

SEX PISTOLS
Anarchy in the U.K./I Wanna Be Me (EMI)
  Everyone should have this by now, it really is a classic and it blew away any doubts about the Sex Pistols' credibility in my mind at least. Is it really 38 in the National charts, and 27 in the NME charts? (*Ripped and Torn* #2, January 1977)

The fanzine record reviews remind us that for every group with the high profile of the Sex Pistols or the Clash there are dozens of groups that formed, recorded, and disappeared. The fanzines are an invaluable source of information on obscure bands, songs, and performances by groups that never received mass-media exposure or international attention.

Punk humor, as exhibited in the fanzines, is another example of shared values in the punk community and an indication of the cohesiveness of punk culture. Characterized by outrageousness in graphics and content, it was designed not only to entertain the readership, but to alienate the general public. *Punk* #1 features sexist humor ("Cars and Girls"), and scatological humor ("Joe"). In *Punk* #3 we find examples of black humor ("Father No's Best"), antireligious humor ("10 Warning Signs of Blessedness"), and a bizarre piece by Legs McNeil entitled "A Story to Fill Space," in which he describes throwing up on a subway.

Finally, the fanzines served as a forum for the exchange of philosophical ideas within the punk community. Feature articles are often devoted to expositions, contributed by fans and staff alike, concerning various aspects of the punk aesthetic and its relationship to society as a whole. The best example of this can be found in *Sniffin' Glue* #11:

O! Nothing Earthly . . .—Poe

THE SCENE/HOW I see it: Since the late 60s there has been a generally stagnant and incestuous rock n roll industrial complex, albeit with a few outposts of creativity, (we all know who they were, no need for lists of names). Inbreeding has resulted in music/genetic debility and instability. BUT: In the last couple of years, in New York/London particularly, there has been a sudden cell regeneration, via fresh input. HOWEVER: This does not represent an entirely unified movement, which in some ways is good because, a) variety is the spice of life, and b) different strokes for different folks is a fair maxim. IN NEW YORK: Musicianship is mostly of a higher standard, group members older and more affluent, and therefore less interested in "social protest" than in art/music. They create these in much more varied formats/patterns than in LONDON: Where, due to socio/economic conditions, the music is younger, badly played (mostly), and overtly political. A lot of English kids are scornful of the Americans' artiness, which they see as student dilettantism, unconnected with real life. However, this is where they miss the point. Groups like the Clash are operating on a straightforward political level, which is a lower strata of thought, an elaboration of the "who ate my porridge" argument. They represent something which those in power have seen before, and can be easily assimilated, controlled, dealt with and even incorporated into existing structures. (There's always a place for a token revolutionary). People like Patti Smith Group, Television, etc., are infinitely more threatening to the current social orders, because they turn their backs on them to present symbolist visions of ecstacy, the desire to become God. This is a subtler magic, and one that is incomprehensible to those in control of purely physical realities.

If Clash win their struggle, all they'll have is a bigger slice of cake.

If Television/Smith Group win theirs, they'll be beyond all that, heading for the stars.

I know which idea excites ME more.

recommended reading: Anything by Colin Wilson, especially "The Outsider" and "Introduction to the New Existentialism." (Robertson, July 1977)

Form and content combine in the fanzines to create a striking visual and psychological impact. With their chaotic appearance, subversive graphics, offensive subject matter, aggressive antisocial tone, and liberal use of profanities and off-color humor, they provide definition to the concept of the punk aesthetic. As a forum for the exchange of information, opinion, and philosophy, they served as a focal point for the energies of the punk community. They were a unifying element, reinforcing shared values among punks. As a source of primary data concerning punk bands, rock stars, and performances they are extremely valuable. Along with music and fashion they played a pivotal role in establishing this unique and dynamic youth subculture.

Conclusion

The truth is that punk rock is a phrase that has been around at least since the beginning of the Seventies, and what it at bottom means is rock 'n' roll in its most basic, primitive form. In other words, punk rock has existed throughout the history of rock 'n' roll, they just didn't call it that. In the Fifties, when rock 'n' roll was . . . new . . . the media had a field day. This stuff was derided mercilessly, it was called "unmusical," it was blamed for juvenile delinquency, sexual depravity . . . if not the demise of Western civilization as a whole. It was said that the musicians could not play their instuments; in large part, by any conventional standards (what they used to call "good" music), this was true. Does that matter now to the people who are still listening to those classic oldies twenty years later? It was said that the singers could not sing, by any previous "legitimate" musical standard; this was also true. It was written off nearly everywhere as a load of garbage that would come and go within a year's time, a fad like the hula hoop.

Is any of this beginning to sound vaguely familiar?

Lester Bangs, *Blondie*

The development of punk rock has been traced, from the seminal influence of Lou Reed and the Velvet Underground, through the experiments in outrageous fashion and performance of David Bowie and the New York Dolls, to the proto-punk CBGB scene. The influence of New York underground rock, as a source of role models and musical inspiration, is clear. By concentrating on New York underground rock I have documented the key elements in the evolution of the punk style and established conclusively their relationships to one another.

In describing the evolution of the punk style, one must resist the temptation to be overly analytical and pedantic about a subject which is by its very nature somewhat spontaneous and "nonserious." The spirit with which the music is conceived and created can be buried and lost in theoretical scholarly analysis. No matter what else rock-and-roll, in its various manifestations, is, it is essentially a youth-oriented popular entertainment.

"Rock 'n' roll is supposed to be fun. You remember fun don'tcha? You're supposed to enjoy it" (Rotten quoted in Boston, 1978, 8). Johnny Rotten never had any illusions about the Sex Pistols being an actual political force, or his ability to change society significantly in any meaningful way: "The Pistols are presenting one alternative to apathy and if you don't like it that's just too bad. It's not political anarchy . . . it's musical anarchy" (Rotten quoted in Boston 1978, 22). As we have seen, the Sex Pistols were a conscious reaction against the pretentions to art and respectability of mainstream rock musicians of the 1970s. In an interview with Tom Snyder in 1981 Rotten explained:

> There should be no difference between who's on stage and who's in the audience. We've tried very hard to break down those barriers . . . we were totally honest. We went on stage and we were totally honest. We weren't saying "Look at me. I'm great. I'm a superstar." We weren't saying particularly anything. We were going there and playing our music and anything could have happened when we were on stage. (reprinted from *Punk* Special Edition 1981, 51)

If their goals were indeed just to entertain and have fun they seem to have been a success. They created excitement for themselves and their fans. If they represented a rebellion against anything, it was against teenage apathy and boredom. The facts of their working-class backgrounds gave their music social and political overtones which served as a rallying point for their followers. People identified with this message of rage against the status quo and displayed their empathy by adopting the punk lifestyle. The development of the punk aesthetic into a significant subculture attests to the fact that they spoke for a whole generation of disaffected youth.

When it became clear to the band that the Sex Pistols were on the brink of achieving the superstar status that they had initially condemned as representative of all that was wrong with the music industry, they broke up the band. Part of this process of the self-destruction of the Sex Pistols continued with Johnny Rotten's attempts to demythologize the band and disclaim all theories that they were anything but a loud rock-and-roll band. "Politics?," he would say years later in the 1980s. "The Sex Pistols weren't into politics. The Sex Pistols were a fiasco. A farce" (Miller, ed. 1980, 426). And perhaps there is an element of truth in what he says. Perhaps all they were really about was having a good time. As Pete Townshend of the Who has said, "Rock won't eliminate your problems. But it will let you sort of dance all over them" (Miller, ed. 1980, 286).

Despite Rotten's claims to the contrary, however, the Sex Pistols, and the punk movement they so clearly exemplified, were an important social and political phenomenon. There was no change in government—punks didn't really care about that—and there are still spiritually deadening working-class slums in Britain teeming with bored, angry youths. This seems to be an intractable problem, an unfortunate fact of modern society. But in drawing attention to these problems and giving voice to this feeling of injustice and despair rampant among their peers, the Sex Pistols, and the punks in general, are worthy of our attention. Moreover, the words to "God Save the Queen"—"the fascist regime, they made you a moron . . . there is no future in England's dreaming"—even if spoken in jest, are a definite political statement. It is a characteristic of the stability of the democracy in Great Britain that not only are people permitted to speak like this in public, but in the end, nothing in the nature of change actually comes of it.

Artistically, on the other hand, the Sex Pistols and the punk movement have had a profound effect on the culture of their times. The repercussions of the punk style can still be seen today in music and fashion. The British punk movement has evolved extensively since the late 1970s—branching out, over-lapping with other genres, and being absorbed by a large number of musical styles internationally. As early as 1975—shortly after the formation of the Sex Pistols—an American punk movement had already begun to emerge, closely imitating its British predecessor. Bands and clubs, along with the attending fashion, graphics, and aggressive attitude, sprang up in cities across the country.

In New York the A7 club was the most notable for its importation of punk fashion as a ready-made style. In operation from 1979 to 1983, it attracted a clientele of musicians and fans who embraced the outward appearances of punk, but who were nonetheless far removed from, or even ignorant of, the underlying causes and philosophies which catalyzed the British movement. Moreover, punk began to be assimilated with American musical trends. For instance, New York bands such as the Contortions and Teenage Jesus and the Jerks absorbed punk into a jazz-based idiom; the Dictators combined punk and heavy metal. Others, like the Cleveland-based Devo, translated the idea of "No Future" into a presentation of the performer as human robot. Reggae, rockabilly, and New York underground rock were also American genres which absorbed elements of British punk.

Nowhere is the rapidly cyclical nature of rock-and-roll history more evident than in the series of events surrounding punk rock. Punk broke all the rules and declared war on all previously existing musical trends and rules of social behavior. Rebelling against established musical trends and social mores, punk quickly became a tradition in itself—a movement with highly predictable stylistic elements. By 1981, just six years after the formation of the Sex Pistols, a new generation of performers had already begun to assert an identity distinct from the established punk style.

A variety of musical styles emerged both as a reaction against, and a progression from, punk rock. Themes such as commercial appeal, technical expertise, and lyrical content concerned with romantic love began to reappear. In contrast to punk's anthem of "No Future," lyrics became more markedly optimistic and romantic in tone. Retaining the punk idea of fashion as social/ political statement, while rejecting its preoccupation with pessimism and amateur status, many new bands acquired a degree of respectability within mainstream culture that punk bands had not. The music became more technically polished, with complex rhythms and intricate melodies.

As the original impetus of punk began to wane, the commercialization of punk and its absorption into mainstream culture became apparent. As fashions and music billed as "punk" began to appear in Harrod's, Bloomingdale's, and Radio City Music Hall, punk was robbed of its subversive edge. There is no more efficient means of rendering a subversive movement impotent than to present it as high fashion and declare it safe for mainstream consumption. By downplaying its rebellious nature, the original punk message became trivialized and the symbols that had served as rallying points and as a focus for disaffected youth were destroyed.

Here we come full circle in the evolution of rock-and-roll as seen through the lens of punk. Emerging as the antithesis of the conservative musical climate of the 1970s, punk was quickly absorbed and exploited by the very elements against which it rebelled. Undoubtedly a new generation of performers will soon find an aesthetic and philosophical means of rebelling against the now commercial state of rock, just as punks did in the last decade.

It is clear that the history of punk rock bears a close resemblance to particular movements of the avant-garde of the twentieth century. Correlations between punk and specific movements in the historical avant-garde have been discussed in detail in the introduction. This comparison shows that punk and the historical avant-garde have a common impetus: both are, at their most basic, reactions against traditional theories and techniques of art, as well as against the society which produces them. Both genres asserted unique identities in an attempt to voice what they considered to be a more pertinent view of the world than that reflected by traditional values. It is not surprising that, as a result of these common goals, punk and the historical avant-garde incorporated many of the same revolutionary tactics: unusual fashions; the blurring of boundaries between art and everyday life; juxtapositions of seemingly disparate objects and behaviors; intentional provocation of the audience; use of untrained performers; and drastic reorganization (or disorganization) of accepted performance styles and procedures.

While these similarities are instructive to an analytical study of punk culture, it is important to keep in mind that punk rock is not considered to be a charter member of the historical avant-garde per se. The historical avant-garde refers to a series of movements created by aspiring artists and studied most closely by art historians. Members of the historical avant-garde "isms" (e.g., symbolism, futurism, dadaism, expressionism) identify themselves primarily as artists, and their identity as members of their respective movements is intricately tied to their awareness of their place in art history.

While punk shares many revolutionary tactics with the avant-garde, and in some cases expresses a conscious alliance with it, it is categorically distinct. Punk was created by youths who identified themselves, not primarily as artists, but as bored working-class youths looking for entertainment. Most had neither formal training in art history nor a consciousness of the similarities between their rebellious tactics and those of earlier avant-garde movements. Punk is now, for the most part, attracting the scholarly attention of sociologists and popular culture specialists rather than art historians.

Punk culture, although defined through a configuration of music, fashion, graphics, literary style, philosophy, and personal demeanor, was primarily musically oriented. Punk did not set out to instigate an interdisciplinary artistic movement. The historical avant-garde, on the other hand, is defined in part by its interest in establishing an interdisciplinary approach to art.

While the primary concern of the avant-garde is artistic rebellion, the primary concern of punk, like other youth subcultures, is social rebellion. Though the two concerns are closely related and often difficult to consider as separate intentions, clearly the avant-garde is most self-consciously artistic, while punk is most self-consciously proletarian.

Appendix

Sheet Music

ANARCHY IN THE U.K.

Words & Music by Johnny Rotten, Paul Cook, Steve Jones, and Glen Matlock

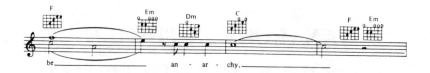

be_____ an - ar - chy,_____

No dogs - body
It's
in the city
Guitar solo
3 times

D.S.

3. How

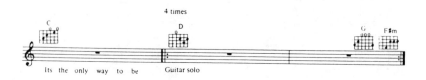

4 times

Its the only way to be
Guitar solo

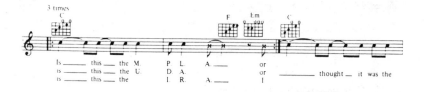

3 times

Is _____ this ___ the M. P. L. A. _____ or
is _____ this ___ the U. D. A. _____ or _____ thought _ it was the
is _____ this ___ the I. R. A. _____ I

GOD SAVE THE QUEEN

Words & Music by Johnny Rotten, Paul Cook, Steve Jones, and Glen Matlock

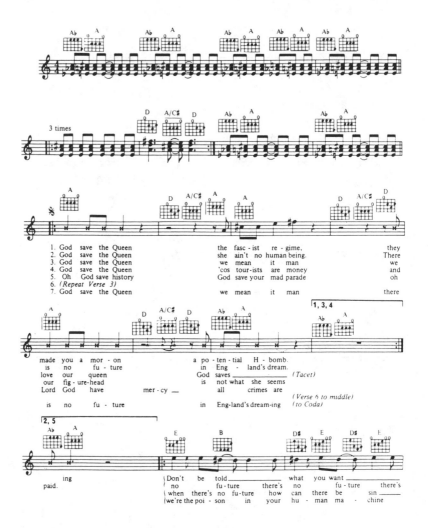

1. God save the Queen   the fasc-ist re-gime,   they
2. God save the Queen   she ain't no human being.   There
3. God save the Queen   we mean it man   we
4. God save the Queen   'cos tour-ists are money   and
5. Oh God save history   God save your mad parade   oh
6. *(Repeat Verse 3)*
7. God save the Queen   we mean it man   there

made you a mor-on   a po-ten-tial H - bomb.
is no fu-ture   in Eng - land's dream.
love our queen   God saves _____ *(Tacet)*
our fig-ure-head   is not what she seems
Lord God have   mer-cy ___   all crimes are   *(Verse 6 to middle)*

is no fu-ture   in Eng-land's dream-ing   *(to Coda)*

|2, 5

ing
paid.

\{ Don't be told _____ what you want _____
\{ no fu-ture there's no fu-ture there's
\{ when there's no fu-ture how can there be sin _____
\{ we're the poi-son in your hu-man ma-chine

no   don't   be   told _____ what you need.   There's   you _____
no   fu - ture for   you
we're   the   flow - ers   in   the   dust - bin
we're   the   fu - ture   you're future

MIDDLE

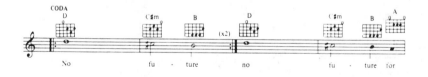

CODA

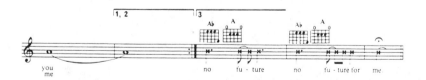

No   fu - ture   no   fu - ture for

you   no   fu - ture   no   fu - ture for   me
me

PRETTY VACANT

Words & Music by Johnny Rotten, Paul Cook, Steve Jones, and Glen Matlock

we're va - cant _____ Oh va - cant _____ Don't
a

va - cant _____ Oh we're so pret - ty oh _____ so pret - ty

Ah but now

and we don't care. _____

There's We're pret - ty _____

a- pret-ty va - cant. _____ We're we don't care. _____

PERSONALITY CRISIS

Words by David Johansen; Music by Johnny Thunders

ADDITIONAL LYRICS

2. Now you're trying to be something, now you gotta do something,
   Wanna be someone who counts.
   But you're thinking 'bout the times you did,
   They took every ounce.
   Well, it's sure got to be a shame,
   When you start to scream and shout.
   You got to contradict all these times
   You butterflied about (you was butterflyin').
   'Bout a personality crisis . . . *(To Chorus)*

3. Now with all the crossing fate that mother nature sends,
   Your mirror's getting jammed up with all your friends.
   That's personality, when every scene starts to blend.
   Personality, when your mind starts to blend.
   You've got so much personality you're flashing
   On the friend of a friend of a friend of a friend.
   Personality, wondering how celebrities ever mend
   (Looking fine on television). . . *(To Chorus)*

Additional lyric for fade

   A personality crisis is no crime.
   It's just a personality crisis, please don't sigh.
   Because all the personality, all the personality . . .

Notes

Preface

1. In any discussion of music there is always a difficulty in describing in words the qualities of what is essentially a nonverbal medium. Adjectives used in discussing a particular musical composition refer to the feeling the music gives us, or some imaginary impartial "average" listener, rather than the actual sound itself. If we say that a work is beautiful, lilting, sensuous, exciting, etc., we are in effect anthropomorphizing what is basically an emotionless mathematical formula. That is to say, we are attempting to translate into human terms that which is a function of the sciences of physics and neurobiology. This is especially true in a discussion of punk rock. I use terms like raw, harsh, brutal, savage, hard, driving, unrelenting, ear-splitting, etc., to suggest the mood and texture of the music, but in doing so, I am fully aware of the imprecise nature of these descriptions and the necessarily subjective judgements involved. As will be seen from the newspaper articles and journals I quote, and the interviews I have conducted, I am not alone in addressing this dilemma. Moreover, attempts to resolve this issue by using the terms associated with classical music and classical music theory prove wholly inadequate. Does it help to refer to the tempo of "Anarchy in the U.K." (Sex Pistols 1976) as prestissimo (very fast), or the meter as quadruple meter, or in 4/4 time? Paul Cooper's *Perspectives in Music Theory* makes reference to "'motor rhythm'. . . a recently coined term which describes constant motion in one or several parts." (1974, 37). This does not, I believe, express the driving force or hypnotic pull of a typical Sex Pistols song. Describing punk-rock music in terms of stringendo (pressing onward), accelerando (gradually quickening in speed), affretando (hurrying), forte (loud), fortissimo (very loud), forza (force, strength), marziale (martial), pesante (heavy), serio (serious), sostenuto (sustained), or sforzando (forcing out, strongly accented), does not help us to truly understand the music in question. Perhaps it is necessary for one to be present at one of these punk performances to appreciate fully the implications of terms such as "wall of noise," "threshold of pain," or "musical chaos." In lieu of such firsthand experience, the reader, unfortunately, must be content with the images and feelings that are suggested by these emotionally charged yet vague and imprecise adjectives. I will, however, in the course of discussing individual bands and songs, attempt to thresh out these descriptions with sheet music and taped material in order to afford the reader a broader perspective in the understanding of style in punk-rock music.

Introduction

1. This description is Michael Kirby's, from his course "History of Avant-Garde Performance," New York University, Department of Performance Studies, fall 1981.

2. Ibid.

3. In quoted material I have left references to punk, new wave, street rock, etc. unaltered, though they are often inconsistent with my definitions of punk and underground rock.

Chapter 1

1. Merseybeat is a term which refers to a rock-and-roll movement centered in Liverpool, England between 1964 and 1966. Taking its name from the Mersey river which runs through the city of Liverpool, Merseybeat is epitomized by such bands as Gary and the Pacemakers, Billy J. Kramer and the Dakotas, and Herman's Hermits. According to *The Rolling Stone Encyclopedia of Rock & Roll*, Merseybeat was first inspired by the international success of the Beatles who originated in Liverpool, and is noted for its "jangly guitars, pleasant melodies, immaculate vocal harmonies, and a general air of teenage romantic innocence" (Pareles and Romanowski 1983, 65). Therefore the term "Mock Merseybeat" infers a simulation of these qualities and their British origins in rock-music style.

2. A few Velvet Underground songs, such as "European Son" (1967) and "Sister Ray" (1968), were written in collaboration with Cale, Morrison, and Tucker.

3. *Billboard* magazine first appeared in 1894. *Billboard* has published weekly national popular music charts since 1940. Between 1940 and 1955 the *Billboard* chart fluctuated between a top ten and top thirty listing of record singles. From 1955 to 1958, *Billboard* published a variety of Top 100 charts, ranking records on such criteria as best sellers in stores, most frequently played by disc jockeys, and most frequently played on juke boxes. On 4 August 1958, *Billboard* introduced a new chart, the Hot 100, which consolidated information from their other charts. This has become the American record industry's definitive source for popular record chart data. *The Billboard Pop Annual*, compiled by Joel Whitburn in 1982, rates the Hot 100 singles on an annual rather than a weekly basis. Unless otherwise noted, this is the source cited for all United States popular song ratings.

4. "I'm a Believer" was ranked number one single of the year on the *Billboard* chart; "Heroin" was not ranked.

5. *The McGraw-Hill Encyclopedia of Science and Technology* defines decibel as: "A logarithmic unit used to express the magnitude of a change in level of power, voltage, current, or sound intensity. A decibel (dB) is 1/10 bel" (1982, vol. 4, p. 56). *McGraw-Hill* gives the following decibel ratings to common sounds: whisper, 20 dB; quiet office, 30 dB; ordinary conversation, 45 dB; street noises, 65 dB; machinery, 80 dB; truck, 100 dB; jet plane, 120 dB (vol. 7, p. 812). Louder rock-and-roll bands are known to reach 120 dB during live performance, putting them in the range of a jet engine.

6. Little has been written about these mixed-media shows. In early 1966 the Velvet Underground was virtually unknown to people outside the Warhol circle. The band had been together for only two months, had given only a few performances, and were as yet unrecorded. Though Warhol's work in painting and film was extensively documented, his live performances were almost completely ignored by both journalists and scholars. Therefore the descriptions of Warhol's mixed-media events are based on the few written accounts available on the subject, and on personal interviews I conducted with participants and audience members.

7. *Billboard* charts rate albums on a one to two hundred basis, as opposed to single songs which are rated on a one to one hundred basis.

8. Precise statistics of record sales are recording industry trade secrets. The only information available to the general public concerning the number of records sold is whether or not a record

attained gold or platinum status. Gold status means that, for singles, the record sold one million copies or more; for albums, the record made a profit of one million dollars or more (based from 1958 to 1968 on 50% of the list price, and from 1968 to the present on 33.5% of the list price). Platinum status means that, for singles, the record sold two million copies or more; for albums, the record sold one million copies or more. The Record Industry Association of America began certifying gold records in 1958, and platinum records in 1976. These certifications are now the definitive source for popular record chart data.

9. The last *Exploding Plastic Inevitable* performance did not mark the end of the Velvet Underground, though it was the first of a series of events which eventually led to the band's dissolution. After the breakup of the *Exploding Plastic Inevitable* in May 1967, Nico left the Velvet Underground to pursue a solo career. Between May 1967 and June 1970 the Velvet Underground toured extensively outside New York City and recorded three albums: *White Light/White Heat* (1967), *The Velvet Underground* (1969), and *Loaded* (1970). Although none of these albums made *Billboard* or other national charts, they were important in maintaining the Velvet Underground's following, and are among the few documentations of Velvet Underground music, along with Warhol films and two albums of live performance tapes released after the group disbanded: *Live at Max's Kansas City* (1972) and *Live 1969* (1974).

    John Cale left the Velvet Underground in September 1968 to continue his experiments with classical music. He was replaced by bassist Doug Yule, former member of a Boston-based band named the Glass Menagerie. In August 1970 Reed left the Velvet Underground in order to pursue a solo career. Walter Powers joined the band on bass and Doug Yule took Reed's place as lead singer. Although the resulting lineup—Morrison, Tucker, Yule, Powers—continued to perform Velvet Underground material (no new songs were written for the band after Reed's departure) for over a year, both in New York City and on tour, the original impetus and vitality of the band ware gone, and audiences lost interest in the group. According to Reed: "It was a process of elimination from the start. First no more Andy, then no more Nico, then no more John, then no more Velvet Underground" (Bockris and Malanga 1983, 124).

10. The influence of fanzines on the evolution of punk-rock style will be more thoroughly discussed in chapters 4 and 5.

Chapter 2

1. As noted in the Preface, underground rock is a term I use in reference to bands self-consciously aligned with noncommercial popular music trends. More specifically, it refers to New York City bands supported by cult followings developed through live performances at local nightclubs rather than recording contracts and mass-media hype.

2. According to Harvey Rachlin in *The Encyclopedia of the Recording Industry*, radio programming is determined by several factors: chart ratings of particular recordings, radio station program director and music director recommendations, and disc jockey selections (1981, 312). In light of the varying programming policies of radio stations throughout the United States, I use the term "frequent radio play" to refer to songs which receive at least twice-daily play.

3. Bowie's commercial success at this time is evidenced by the following: (1) *The Rise and Fall of Ziggy Stardust and the Spiders from Mars* rated number seventy-five on the *Billboard* charts in 1972 and sold over one million copies; (2) Bowie launched a series of extensive international tours playing to sold-out concert halls often seating 15,000 or more fans.

4. Two other changes in personnel took place during the New York Dolls' career: in November 1972 Billy Murcia was replaced by Jerry Nolan; from December 1972 to April 1975 Peter Jordan intermittently replaced Arthur Kane.

5. None of the New York Dolls had received formal musical training. Though their technical abilities improved markedly over their three-year career through trial-and-error, their early performances were noted for a lack of accuracy and precision (Miller 1976, 419; Naha 1973, 10; Nelson 1975, 30; Taylor 1974, 20).

6. Although both New York Dolls albums (barely) made the *Billboard* charts (out of a possible 200 record rating *The New York Dolls* made number 116 in 1973; *Too Much Too Soon* made number 167 in 1974), sales figures were not high enough to warrant certification by the Record Industry Association of America of exact numbers of records sold.

7. Teddy boys, or teds, are members of a British youth culture which emerged in the 1950s. They are known for their fashion sensibility which revolves around the wearing of Edwardian suits, and clothing reminiscent of the American West. Teddy boys will be discussed in more detail in chapter 4.

8. Rockers are members of a British youth culture which emerged in the 1960s. They are known for their overtly masculine "streetwise" fashions which incorporated leather jackets and motorcycle-gang appearance. Rockers will be discussed in more detail in chapter 4.

9. No precise records of New York Dolls performances exist from this period. However, according to *Village Voice* performance listings (3 March 1975, 114) the band performed in New York at the Little Hippodrome Theatre on 27 February 1975. Also, according to Pete Frame (1980, 27), the band gave a series of performances in Florida in April 1975.

Chapter 3

1. Manhattan's East Village is a neighborhood bounded by 14th Street on the north, the East River on the east, Houston Street on the south, and Broadway on the west.

2. Skid Row is a colloquial term defined in *Webster's New Universal Unabridged Dictionary* as: "A section of a city frequented by hobos, vagrants, derelicts, etc." (1983). In New York, Skid Row is a common reference to the Bowery, a street located in Manhattan's East Village.

3. In 1974, Patti Smith published a collection of poems entitled *Babel,* printed in New York by G.P. Putnam's Sons.

4. After the appearance of only sixteen issues, *Punk* magazine ceased publication in August 1979 due to financial troubles (though in April 1981 one issue was printed in an unsuccessful attempt to revive the magazine).

Chapter 4

1. In quotations from fanzines and other printed matter generated by the punk movement I have made no attempt to correct grammatical errors, misspellings, or typing errors. These aspects of the quotations are useful in giving the reader firsthand experience of the informal writing and publication styles of these sources.

2. *Labour Force Statistics 1964–1984* (1986) shows that the unemployment rate for 16–24-year-olds in Britain rose steadily during this period. Between 1974 and 1976 the rate more than tripled, leaping from 3.5% to 11.8%.

3. *Labour Force Statistics Yearbook 1977* (1977) shows that the consumer price index in Britain rose from 148.4 in 1974 to 214.9 in 1976. The base for these statistics is $100 =$ the consumer

price index in 1970. According to *The Dictionary of Business and Economics,* the consumer price index uses

> the retail prices of about 400 goods and services sold in a large number of cities across the country. [It] weights products by their importance (in terms of the dollar value of purchases, reflecting their importance in the individual consumer's budget) and compares prices to those of a selected base year, expressing current prices as a percentage of prices in the base year. The main components of the consumer price index are housing, food and beverages, transportation, clothing, and medical care. (1977, 99)

4. While the youth unemployment rate did not reach 35% in 1977, this forecast is a clear indication of the pessimistic outlook caused by the sharp rise in unemployment during this period.

5. Police files of the criminal records of members of the the Sex Pistols show the following offenses. John Lydon (Johnny Rotten): possession of amphetamine sulphate. John Beverly (Sid Vicious): assault of two policemen, criminal damage, possession of offensive weapon (flick knife), assault of policeman, taking of ford transit, destroying policeman's handset. Paul Cook: stealing property worth £900 sterling, small theft. Steve Jones: breaking and entering store (£143 sterling stolen), stealing eight ignition keys, taking and driving away vehicle, use of motor vehicle when under age (no insurance or license), damaging plate glass window, drunk and disorderly, vagrancy act charge (reprinted from Stevenson 1978, 56).

6. Rotten also makes reference to his criminal background in an interview with Mary Harron in the March 1977 issue of *Punk* magazine (vol. 1, no. 8, p. 14).

7. Fanzines were small, handmade, photocopied publications passed at the street level among fans of local bands. They provided a network of communication concerning performances, documented the careers of punk bands like the Sex Pistols, and provided a network of philosophical exchange. They were an alternative to publications like the *Rolling Stone* and the *New Musical Express,* which catered to the tastes of mainstream rock culture.

8. Thames Television refused my request for a copy of the tape, or for a transcript of the interview. However, an excerpt of the interview was recorded on the album *Sex Pistols: We've Cum for Your Children,* Skyclad Recording Company, 1988.

Bibliography

Books

Ammer, Christine and Ammer, Dean S. *Dictionary of Business and Economics.* New York: Free Press, 1984.

Anscombe, Isabelle and Blair, Dike. *Punk.* New York: Urizen Books, 1978.

Apollonio, Umbro, ed. *Futurist Manifestos.* New York: Viking Press, 1970.

Baker, Glenn A. and Coupe, Stuart. *The New Music.* New York: Harmony Books, 1981.

Bangs, Lester. *Blondie.* New York: Delilah Communications, 1980.

Barnes, Richard. *Mods!* London: Eel Pie Publishing, 1979.

Belsito, Peter and Davis, Bob. *Hardcore California: A History of Punk and New Wave.* San Francisco: Last Gasp, 1983.

Belsito, Peter; Davis, Bob; and Kester, Marian. *Street Art: The Punk Poster in San Francisco 1977–1981.* San Francisco: Last Gasp, 1981.

Belz, Carl. *The Story of Rock.* New York: Oxford University Press, 1972.

Benamou, Michel and Caramello, Charles, eds. *Performance in Postmodern Culture.* Madison, Wis.: Coda Press, 1977.

Bergman, Billy and Horn, Richard. *Recombinant Do-Re-Mi: Frontiers of the Rock Era.* New York: Quill, 1985.

Birch, Ian. *The Book with No Name.* London: Omnibus Press, 1981.

Bladow, Janel and Ivins, Mark. *Primal Punk.* New York: Halftone Press, 1982.

Bockris, Victor and Malanga, Gerard. *Uptight: The Velvet Underground Story.* London: Omnibus Press, 1983.

Bockris, Victor; Harry, Debbie; and Stein, Chris. *Making Tracks: The Making of Blondie.* New York: Dell Publishing, 1982.

Boston, Virginia. *Punk Rock.* New York: Penguin Books, 1978.

Brake, Mike. *The Sociology of Youth Culture and Youth Subcultures.* London: Routledge & Kegan Paul, 1980.

Brown, Curtis F. *Star-Spangled Kitch.* New York: Universe Books, 1975.

Burchill, Julie and Parsons, Tony. *The Boy Looked at Johnny.* London: Pluto Press, 1978.

Carr, Roy and Murray, Charles Shaar. *Bowie.* New York: Avon Books, 1981.

Carson, Tom. *Twisted Kicks.* Glen Ellen, Calif.: Entwhistle Books, 1981.

Castellini, John. *Rudiments of Music.* New York: W.W. Norton and Co., 1962.

Clapton, Diana. *Lou Reed and the Velvet Underground.* New York: Proteus Books, 1982.

Cohen, Scott. *Boy George.* New York: Berkley Books, 1984.

Coon, Caroline. *1988: The New Wave Punk Rock Explosion.* London: Omnibus Press, 1977.

Cooper, Paul. *Perspectives in Music Theory: An Historical-Analytical Approach.* New York: Dodd, Mead and Co., 1974.

Copland, Aaron. *The New Music: 1900–1960.* New York: W.W. Norton & Co., 1968.

Dietrich, Jo. *Boy George and the Culture Club.* Port Chester, N. Y.: Cherry Lane Books, 1984.

Ehrenstein, David and Reed, Bill. *Rock on Film.* New York: Delilah Books, 1982.

Elson, Howard. *Early Rockers.* New York: Proteus Books, 1982.

Filley, Patrick, et al., eds. *Rolling Stone Rock Almanac: The Chronicles of Rock & Roll.* New York: MacMillan Publishing Co., 1983.

Fitzgerald, f-Stop. *Weird Angle.* San Francisco, Calif.: Post-Contemporary Productions, 1982.

Foster, Hal, ed. *The Anti-Aesthetic: Essays on Postmodern Culture.* Port Townsend, Wash.: Bay Press, 1983.

Frame, Pete. *Pete Frame's Rock Family Trees.* London: Omnibus Press, 1980.

————. *Pete Frame's Rock Family Trees Volume II.* London: Omnibus Press, 1983.

Gans, David. *Talking Heads.* New York: Avon Books, 1985.

Geertz, Clifford. *The Interpretation of Cultures.* New York: Basic Books, 1973.

Gerald, Howard, ed. *The Sixties.* New York: Pocket Press, 1982.

Goldberg, RoseLee. *Performance: Live Art 1909 to the Present.* New York: Harry N. Abrams, 1979.

Hager, Steven. *Art after Midnight.* New York: St. Martin's Press, 1986.

Hanel, Ed, ed. *The Essential Guide to Rock Books.* London: Omnibus Press, 1983.

Hannah, Judith Lynne. *The Performer-Audience Connection: Emotion to Metaphor in Dance and Society.* Austin, Tex.: University of Texas Press, 1983.

————. *To Dance Is Human: A Theory of Nonverbal Communication.* Austin, Tex.: University of Texas Press, 1979.

Harris, Heather. *Rock 'n' Roll: Punk New Wave.* London: Almo Publications, 1978.

Hebdige, Dick. *Subculture: The Meaning of Style.* London: Methuen and Co., 1979.

Hendler, Herb. *Year by Year in the Rock Era.* Westport, Conn.: Greenwood Press, 1983.

Hennessy, Val. *In the Gutter.* London: Quartet Books, 1978.

Herman, Gary. *Rock 'n' Roll Babylon.* New York: Perigee Books, 1982.

Hounsome, Terry. *The New Rock Record.* New York: Facts on File Publications, 1981.

Jakubowski, Maxim, ed. *Who's Who in Rock Video.* London: Zomba Books, 1983.

Johnson, Garry. *Oi: A View From the Dead-End of the Street.* Manchester: Babylon Books, ca. 1982.

Kirby, Michael. *Futurist Performance.* New York: E.P. Dutton & Co., 1971.

Knight, Nick. *Skinhead.* London: Omnibus Press, 1982.

Labour Force Statistics 1964–1984. Paris: O.E.C.D. Department of Economics and Statistics, 1986.

Labour Force Statistics Yearbook 1977. Paris: O.E.C.D. Department of Economics and Statistics, 1977.

Lindsmith, Alfred R. *Addiction and Opiates.* Chicago: Aldine Publishing Co., 1968.

London, Herbert I. *Closing the Circle: A Cultural History of the Rock Revolution.* Chicago: Nelson-Hall, 1984.

Lunch, Lydia and Cervenka, Exene. *Adulterers Anonymous.* New York: Grove Press, 1982.

Makos, Christopher. *White Trash.* New York: Stonehill Publishing Co., 1977.

Marchbank, Pearce, ed. *Punk Words and Punk Music.* London: Wise Publications, 1982.

Marranca, Bonnie. *Theatre Writings.* New York: Performing Arts Journal Publications, 1984.

Marsh, Dave. *Rock and Roll Confidential Report.* New York: Pantheon Books, 1985.

McGraw-Hill Encyclopedia of Science and Technology, 5th ed. New York: McGraw-Hill Book Co., 1982.

Miles. *Gabba Gabba Hey. The Ramones: An Illustrated Biography.* London: Omnibus Press, 1981.

Miles, ed. *Words and Music: Lou Reed.* London: Wise Publications, 1980.

Miller, Jim, ed. *The Rolling Stone Illustrated History of Rock & Roll.* New York: Random House, 1980.

Muirhead, Bert. *Stiff: The Story of a Record Label 1976–1982*. Poole: Blandford Press, 1983.

Noble, Peter L. *Future Pop: Music for the Eighties*. New York: Putnam Publishing Group, 1983.

Palmer, Myles. *New Wave Explosion*. London: Proteus Books, 1981.

Pareles, Jon and Romanowski, Patricia, eds. *The Rolling Stone Encyclopedia of Rock & Roll*. New York: Rolling Stone Press/Summit Books, 1983.

Polhemus, Ted, ed. *The Body Reader: Social Aspects of the Human Body*. New York: Pantheon Books, 1978.

Polhemus, Ted and Procter, Lynn. *Pop Styles*. London: Vermilion & Co., 1984.

Pop, Iggy and Wehrer, Anne. *I Need More*. New York: Karz-Cohl Publishing, 1980.

Rachlin, Harvey. *The Encyclopedia of the Music Business*. New York: Harper and Row, 1981.

Reese, Krista. *Talking Heads*. London: Proteus Books, 1982.

Robbins, Ira A., ed. *The New Trouser Press Record Guide*. New York: Charles Scribner's Sons, 1985.

Santos, Raye, et al. *X-Capees: A San Francisco Punk Photo Documentary*. San Francisco: Last Gasp, 1981.

Schaffner, Nicholas. *The British Invasion*. New York: McGraw-Hill Book Co., 1983.

Schechner, Richard. *Essays on Performance Theory 1970–1976*. New York: Drama Book Specialists, 1977.

_____ . *The End of Humanism*. New York: Performing Arts Journal Publications, 1982.

Schechner, Richard and Schuman, Mady, eds. *Ritual, Play, and Performance: Readings in the Social Sciences/Theatre*. New York: The Seabury Press, 1976.

Sculatti, Gene, ed. *The Catalog of Cool*. New York: Warner Books, 1982.

Shattuck, Roger. *The Banquet Years*. New York: Vintage Books, 1968.

Simels, Steven. *Gender Chameleons: Androgyny in Rock 'n' Roll*. New York: Timbre Books/Arbor House, 1985.

Smith, Patti. *Babel*. New York: G.P. Putnam's Sons, 1974.

Spungen, Deborah. *And I Don't Want to Live This Life*. New York: Villard Books, 1983.

Steele-Perkins, Chris and Smith, Richard. *The Teds*. London: Travelling Light/Exit, 1979.

Stein, Jean, ed. *Edie: An American Biography*. New York: Dell Publishing Co., 1983.

Stevenson, Ray. *The Sex Pistols File*. London: Omnibus Press, 1978.

Stewart, Tony, ed. *25 Years of Rock 'n' Roll Style*. New York: Delilah Books, 1982.

Talking Heads. London (no further credits).

Thomson, Liz, ed. *New Women in Rock*. New York: Delilah/Putnam, 1982.

Warhol, Andy. *POPism: The Warhol '60s*. New York: Harper and Row, 1980.

West, Mike. *The Velvet Underground and Lou Reed*. Manchester: Babylon Books, 1982.

Whitburn, Joel. *The Billboard Pop Annual 1955–1982*. Menomonee Falls, Wis.: Record Research, 1983.

_____ . *Joel Whitburn's Top Pop Albums: 1955–1985*. Menomonee Falls, Wis.: Record Research, 1985.

Periodicals and Magazines

Ave. E. (unnumbered, undated).

Chainsaw, no. 13, July 1983.

Damage, issue 12/13, June 1981.

Decline of Art, no. 1, 1981.

_____ , no. 2, 1981.

Dry, no. 7, 1981.

_____ , no. 8 (undated).

_____ , no. 11 (undated).

The Face, no. 16, August 1981.
————— , no. 36, April 1983.
————— , no. 38, June 1983
————— , no. 40, August 1983.
————— , no. 44, December 1983.
Flexipop!, issue 6 (undated).
————— , issue 14 (undated).
————— , no. 1 (undated).
————— , no. 3 (undated).
————— , no. 32 (undated).
————— , no. 666 (undated).
Heat, no. 4, October/November 1977.
i-D, no. 12 (undated).
Impulse, vol. 9, nos. 3 and 4, Spring 1982.
Jamming!, no. 14, 1983.
New York Rocker, March 1984.
No Its Not the Sun (unnumbered, undated).
No Mag (unnumbered, undated).
The Poser, issue 6 (undated).
Punk, vol. 1, no. 1, January 1976.
————— , vol. 1, no. 3, April 1976.
————— , vol. 1, no. 4, July 1976.
————— , vol. 1, no. 5, August 1976.
————— , vol. 1, no. 7, February 1977.
————— , vol. 1, no. 8, March 1977.
————— , vol. 1, no. 12, January 1978.
————— , vol. 1, no. 14, May/June 1978.
————— , vol. 1, no. 15, July/August 1978.
————— , Special Edition no. 1, 10 April 1981.
Punk Lives, no. 7 (undated).
Ripped and Torn, no. 2, January 1977.
Sniffin' Glue, no. 3, September 1976.
————— , no. 4, October 1976.
————— , no. 11, July 1977.
Starzone, vol. 1, no. 1, Summer 1981.
Tabloid, no. 5, Winter 1982.
————— , no. 7, Winter 1983.
Tribal Noize, no. 3 (undated).
Tues. Night, no. 2, 6 September 1977.
The Velvet Underground Appreciation Society/What Goes On, nos. 1 and 2, April 1986.
Wet, no. 34, November/December 1981.
ZG, no. 3 (undated).
————— , no. 7 (undated).
————— , no. 8 (undated).
Zig Zag, no. 124, April 1982.

Articles and Unpublished Material

"At Mr. Chow's." *New Yorker*, 14 March 1983, p. 43.
Barol, Bill and Dallas, Rita. "Mad about the Boy." *Newsweek*, 16 May 1983, p. 90.

Battcock, Gregory. "Notes on the Chelsea Girls." *Art Journal,* Summer 1967, p. 363.

Blaylock, William. "Picking the Pockets of Pop." *Time,* 28 November 1983, p. 83.

Brown, Mick. "Punk: Something Rotten in England." *Rolling Stone,* 11 August 1977, p. 15.

Carlsen, Peter and Smith, Philip. "The Next Wave." *Gentlemen's Quarterly,* March 1983, p. 224.

Charlesworth, Chris. "Bowie." *The History of Rock* 7, no. 82 (1983), p. 1624.

Christgau, Georgia. "Is Roger Euster the Meanest Punk in Punk Rock?" *Village Voice,* 30 May 1977, p. 19.

Christgau, Robert. "We Have to Deal with It." *Village Voice,* 9 January 1978, p. 1.

_____ . "Avant-Punk." *Village Voice,* 24 October 1977, p. 57.

Cipnic, Dennis. "Andy Warhol: Iconographer." *Sight and Sound,* Summer 1972, p. 158.

Citron, Atay. "The Interaction among Punk, Performance Art and S&M Theatre." New York: 1982 (unpublished manuscript).

Collins, Nancy. "Boy George." *Rolling Stone,* 7 June 1984, p. 13.

Coon, Caroline. "Anarchy, Venom, Outrage, Fury!" *Melody Maker,* 27 November 1976, p. 33.

Cox, Alex. "1976 and All That: The Rise and Fall of the Blank Generation." *New Musical Express,* 1 February 1986, p. 26.

Curran, Ann. "CMU's Other Andy." *Carnegie-Mellon Magazine,* Spring 1985, p. 12.

D.C.E. "New York Dolls: Glitter and Grace on the Way to the Top." *Caremont Collegian,* 20 March 1974, p. 3.

Diliberto, Gioia. "Invasion of the Gender Blenders." *People Weekly,* 23 April 1984, p. 96.

Edwards, Henry. "Rock and Rouge." *High Fidelity,* October 1973, p. 95.

Ehrenstein, David. "Room Service (the Chelsea Girls)." *Film Culture,* Fall 1966, p. 8.

Emerson, Ken. "Today's Punks Make the Old Punks Sound Mellow." *New York Times Magazine,* 4 December 1977, p. 17.

Erlich, Nancy. "Mott the Hoople/New York Dolls." *Billboard,* 18 August 1973, p. 48.

Fricke, David. "A Boy Named George Breaks Down the Sex Barriers in Rock's Outrageous Culture Club." *People Weekly,* 1 August 1983 p. 86.

Glover, Tony. "New York Dolls and What's It to Ya?" *Rolling Stone,* 13 September 1973, p. 64.

Gluek, Grace. "Syndromes Pop at Delmonico's." *New York Times,* 14 January 1966, p. 36.

_____ . "Warhol's World." *New York Times,* 9 June 1966, sec. E, p. 6.

Goldberg, Michael. "Culture Club Sings for Peace." *Rolling Stone,* 6 December 1984, p. 55.

Goldstein, Richard. "The Possibilities of Punk." *Village Voice,* 10 October 1977, p. 44.

Haas, Charlie. "Two Minute Warnings." *New West,* 30 January 1978, p. 31.

Harrington, Stephanie. "*Inevitable* Explodes on St. Mark's Place." *Village Voice,* 16 June 1966, p. 29.

Harron, Mary. "Punk Is Just Another Word for Nothin' Left to Lose." *Village Voice,* 28 March 1977, p. 54.

Henry, Tricia. "Punk and the Historical Avant-Garde." *Journal of Popular Culture,* Spring 1984.

_____ . "The A-7 Club: A Look at Punk Rock Performance Space." New York, 1982 (unpublished manuscript).

Hume, Martha. "The Rough, Tough Image of Women in Rock." *Daily News,* 27 March 1983, p. 15.

Ingham, Jonh. "Welcome to the (?) Rock Special." *Sounds,* 9 October 1976, p. 22.

_____ . "The Sex Pistols." *Sounds,* 24 April 1976, p. 10.

"Is Boy George Corrupting Our Youth?" *Gainesville Sun Family Weekly,* 1 July 1984, p. 4.

Jones, Jerene. "Boy Oh Boy." *People Weekly,* 23 April 1984, p. 92.

Keating, Robert. "Slamdancing in a Fast City." *Penthouse,* February 1982, p. 77.

Kirby. "The Dolls." *Variety,* 21 June 1972, p. 61.

Lester, Elenore. "So He Stopped Painting Brillo Boxes and Bought a Movie Camera." *New York Times,* 11 December 1966, sec. D, p. 14.

Lhamon, W. T. "Dadapunk." *Bennington Review,* April 1980, p. 39.

Loder, Kurt. "Culture Club: The Boy Behind Britain's Biggest Band." *Rolling Stone,* 17 February 1983, p. 43.

———. "London Calling." *Rolling Stone,* 10 November 1983, p. 17.

Lord, Barry. "Velvet Underground in Hamilton." *Arts Canada,* 24 February 1967, p. 15.

Marsh, Dave. "Kick out the Jams." *Rolling Stone,* 25 August 1977, p. 23.

Mayer, Ira. "Manhattan Clubs Face Bottom Line." *Village Voice,* 5 September 1974, p. 58.

McCormack, Ed. "New York City's Ultra Living Dolls." *Rolling Stone,* 26 October 1972, p. 14.

Miller, Jim, et al. "Rock's New Women." *Newsweek,* 4 March 1985, p. 48.

———. "From Pop to Punk." *Newsweek,* 4 March 1985, p. 52.

Mortifoglio, Richard. "Watch Television." *Village Voice,* 7 July 1975, p. 95.

Naha, Ed. "New York Dolls: Raw Energy, Unpolished and Totally Captivating." *Good Times,* 3 August 1973, p. 10.

Nelson, Paul. "Valley of the New York Dolls." *Village Voice,* 26 May 1975, p. 130.

———. "Johansen's New York Dolls: More Music, Less Flash." *Rolling Stone,* 12 February 1976, p. 102.

O'Hara, Charles. "The Velvet Underground: Pittsburgh, PA 1968." New York, 1984 (unpublished manuscript).

Paisley, Luther. "Growing Up in Public: Lou Reed's Revealing Quest for Maturity." *The History of Rock* 7, no. 82, 1983.

Palmer, Robert. "Punk Rock: 3 English Groups Team for a Concert at Club 57." *New York Times,* 3 September 1979, sec. C, p. 16.

———. "Rock: New Theater Opens with Punk." *New York Times,* 29 December 1977, sec. C, p. 14.

Parsons, Tony. "Punk: Ten Years On." *New Musical Express,* January 1986, p. 1.

"Past Pseudo Punk." *Florida Flambeau,* 30 May 1985, p. 19.

"Pistols Sign EMI Deal." *Sounds,* 16 October 1976, p. 2.

Post, Henry. "Late-Late New York." *New York,* 3 May 1982, p. 22.

Preston, Dick. "Instant Filmmaker." *East Village Other,* 15 November–1 December 1966, p. 16.

———. "Scenes." *Village Voice,* 22 September 1966, p. 28.

———. "Andy's Gang Bang." *East Village Other,* 5 January 1966, p. 12.

"Punk." *The Face,* February/March 1986, p. 70.

Robinson, Lisa. "Punk Rockers Set Off British." *Sun Times,* 26 December 1976, p. 4.

Rock, Mick. "Lou Reed Sees the Future, Darkly." *Rolling Stone,* 26 October 1972, p. 12.

"Rock's New Women." *Newsweek,* 4 March 1985, p. 48.

Rockwell, John. "Experimental Rock Vigorous in Britain." *New York Times,* 14 January 1979, sec. D, p. 33.

———. "Rock: The Punk Circuit." *New York Times,* 26 August 1977, sec. C, p. 4.

———. "The Connections of 'Punk-Jazz.'" *New York Times,* 20 January 1980, sec. D, p. 22.

———. "The Paradox of the Sex Pistols." *New York Times,* 5 February 1978, sec. D, p. 5.

———. "The Punk Scene May Be Waning, But the Clash Carry On." *New York Times,* 9 July 1978, sec. D, p. 7.

———. "When the Punks Meet the Progressives." *New York Times,* 23 October 1977, sec. D, p. 20.

Rose, Frank. "Welcome to the Modern World." *Esquire,* April 1981, p. 29.

Savage, Jon. "What Did You Do on the Jubilee?" *Sounds,* 18 June 1977, p. 1.

"Sex Pistols Record 'Blacked' by Packers." *The Daily Telegraph,* 4 December 1976, p. 3.

Sheehy, Gail. "Playing with Sexual Identity." *Daily News,* 10 August 1984, p. 31.

Shewey, Don. "Culture Club Sounds the Alarm." *Rolling Stone,* 22 November, 1984, p. 73.

Simels, Steve. "The New York Dolls." *Stereo Review,* January 1974, p. 56.

Smith, Howard. "Boy Scouts of Rock." *Village Voice,* 8 May 1978, p. 10.

———. "The Shot That Shattered the Velvet Underground." *Village Voice,* 6 June 1978, p. 1.

_____ . "Punk: Airing the Problems." *Village Voice,* 12 June 1978, p. 26.

Sommer, Sally. "Night in the Slammer." *Village Voice,* 18 January 1983, p. 29.

Sontag, Susan. *Against Interpretation.* 6th ed. New York: Dell Publishing Co., 1964.

Southern, Richard. *The Seven Ages of the Theatre.* New York: Hill and Wang, 1961.

Spungen, Deborah. "Love Me, Kill Me." *Penthouse,* October 1983, p. 57.

Taylor, Barry. "New York Dolls/Elliot Murphy." *Billboard,* 23 March 1974, p. 20.

Tosches, Nick. "Country Punks on the Great Lawn." *Village Voice,* 23 August 1974, p. 58.

Walters, Charley. "Punk: Pretty Vacant Music." *Rolling Stone,* 6 October 1977, p. 103.

Wilcock, John. "A 'High' School of Music and Art." *East Village Other,* 15 April–1 May 1966, p. 5.

_____ . "Other Scenes." *East Village Other,* 15 February 1966, p. 4.

Williams, Richard. "Velvet Underground." *Melody Maker,* 16 October 1971, p. 26.

Willis, Ellen. "Lou Reed." New York: RCA Records, public relations materials, 1986.

Wolcott, James. "The Rise of Punk Rock." *Village Voice,* 1 March 1976, p. 87.

_____ . "We Must Lurch My Lovelies." *Village Voice,* 27 June 1977, p. 44.

_____ ."A Conservative Impulse in the New Rock Underground." *Village Voice,* 18 August 1975, p. 6.

_____ . "The Ramones: Chord Killers." *Village Voice,* 21 July 1975, p. 94.

Zabor, Rafi. "John Lydon's P.I.L." *Musician,* November 1984, p. 13.

Films

Kawalski, Lech, producer/director. *D.O.A.* New York: High Times Films, 1981.

Jarman, Derek, director. *Jubilee.* London: Whaley Malin/Megalovision, 1978.

Spheeris, Penelope, producer/director. *The Decline of Western Civilization.* Los Angeles: Music Media, 1980.

Videotapes

Alpert, Steve, director. *Girl Groups: The Story of a Sound.* Delilah Films, 1983.

Gruen, Bob and Gruen, Nadya. *The New York Dolls: Lookin' for a Kiss.* 1973.

Gruen, Bob. *Lipstick Killers.* 1974.

_____ . *Don Kirshner's Rock Concert: The New York Dolls.* 1974.

Lawrence, Steve, producer. *Rock 'n' Roll of the 80s: A Video History.* MTV Networks, 1985.

Louder, Faster, Shorter. San Francisco, 1978.

McLuhan, Stephanie, producer/director. *Marshall McLuhan: The Man and His Message.* McLuhan Productions, 1984.

Interviews

Blackwood, Tanya. Archivist. Recording Industry Association of America. New York, 5 August 1986.

Carrion, Ricko. Fan. Tallahassee, Fla., 22 March 1986.

Gruen, Bob. Photographer. New York, 15 September 1986.

Hamagami, Louise. Editor, Cinemetric. New York, 5 August 1986.

Hell, Richard. Performer. Tallahassee, Fla., 22 February 1986.

Holmstrom, John. Editor, *Punk* magazine. New York, 13 October 1986; 14 November 1986.

Ivins, Mark. Freelance photographer, author. New York, 14 August 1984; 5 December 1986.

Jordan, Peter. Bass player for the New York Dolls. New York, 24 September 1986; 26 November 1986.

Kostek, M. C. Publisher/editor for *What Goes On* magazine. Stuart, Fla., 3 July 1986 (telephone interview).

Kristal, Hilly. Owner of CBGB. New York, 4 July 1986; 8 October 1986.

Lewis, Daniel. Fan. Cocoa Beach, Fla., 21 August 1986 (telephone interview).

Malanga, Gerard. Photographer and member of *Exploding Plastic Inevitable*. New York, 5 September 1986.

O'Hara, Charles. Fan and member of the Riff Doctors. New York, 21 August 1984; 14 June 1985; 12 October 1986.

Presley, Greg. Assistant Professor of Music, Florida State University. Tallahassee, Fla., 13 April 1986.

Striffler, Mark. Entertainment booking agent, Florida State University. Tallahassee, Fla., 12 January 1986.

Webber, Julian. Fan. New York, 18 February 1982.

Index